# HACK COLLEGE LIKE
# AN ENTREPRENEUR

# HACK COLLEGE LIKE AN ENTREPRENEUR

## ANTONIA LIU

NEW DEGREE PRESS

HACK COLLEGE LIKE AN ENTREPRENEUR

ISBN-13   978-1641370240

*For the seekers who are always looking to learn more, do more, love more, give more, and become more.*

*Special thanks to Tony Robbins, Tim Ferriss, and Gary Vaynerchuk for inspiring me to be a seeker and share what I have learned along the way.*

# CONTENTS

INTRODUCTION ........................................................... 1

HOW TO HACK THIS BOOK .................................... 13

## PART ONE: WHAT TO THINK ABOUT

1. WHY DO YOU DESERVE IT? ................................. 19
2. WHAT IF YOU COULD HAVE ANYTHING? ........................... 23
3. WHAT DO YOU LOVE? ........................................... 29
4. ARE YOU "SO GOOD THAT THEY CAN'T IGNORE YOU"? ... 35
5. WHAT IS YOUR COMPETITIVE ADVANTAGE? ...................... 41
6. 20 QUESTIONS TO "KNOW THYSELF" ........................ 49
7. WHAT DO YOU WANT FROM COLLEGE? ........................... 55
8. HOW CAN YOU OPTIMIZE THE NEXT FOUR YEARS? ......... 61
9. WHY DO YOU WANT TO BECOME AN ENTREPRENEUR? .... 65
10. WHAT PROBLEMS DO YOU WANT TO SOLVE? ................... 71

## PART TWO: WHAT TO LEARN

11. LEADING YOUR OWN SHIP ................................. 77
12. RESOURCEFULNESS ........................................... 87
13. THE SUBTLE ART OF NOT GIVING A F*CK ...................... 95
14. ENJOY LIFE ................................................ 101
15. MEDITATE WITHOUT FALLING ASLEEP ...................... 109
16. WIN THE WAR OVER PROCRASTINATION .................... 115
17. TIME MANAGEMENT ........................................ 121
18. THE IN-DEMAND SUPERPOWER: DEEP WORK ................ 129

19. HOW TO HACK COLLEGE ............................................... 139

20. LEARN ANYTHING FASTER ...............................................147

21. DANCE WITH FEAR ............................................. 153

22. STARTUP 101 ...............................................161

23. ATTRACTION AND PERSUASION ......................... 167

24. RESOURCES TO STAY ON THE EDGE OF
    THE ENTREPRENEURIAL WORLD........................... 173

## PART THREE: WHAT TO DO

25. SET BOLD GOALS............................................... 187

26. SET UP YOUR DAY TO WIN ................................. 193

27. CREATE A STRONG PEER GROUP ....................... 199

28. BUILD ON YOUR STRENGTHS.............................205

29. GET STRONGER, LITERALLY...............................211

30. BE THE HUMBLEST PERSON YOU KNOW ..........................217

31. LISTEN.................................................223

32. FOLLOW WARREN BUFFETT'S A-BOOK-A-DAY DIET........229

33. GO PARTY!...............................................235

34. START SOMETHING, ANYTHING .........................239

35. FAIL FAST, FAIL FORWARD ............................... 247

36. HUSTLE LIKE CRAZY .......................................253

37. CREATE OVERNIGHT SUCCESS ...........................259

38. BUILD A REAL NETWORK...............................265

39. TASTE THE STARTUP WORLD.............................. 273

40. WRITE A BOOK ................................................. 277

ACKNOWLEDGMENTS........................................ 281

APPENDIX ............................................................285

# INTRODUCTION

___

*"Have you ever thought about dropping out of college?"*

*My dinner guest was focused on the noodles in her bowl of soup when I asked her the question. She finished slurping the noodle that was halfway into her mouth and raised her eyes to meet mine.*

*I held eye contact while I waited for her answer.*

*It was a bold question. I knew it when I asked it. I had spent the past months thinking about it constantly. Recent reports put college debt in this country at over $1.4 trillion: almost double the size of all credit card debts combined. Layered on top of that was my feeling that some of my college classes had little value. The balance was tipping.*

*I know I am one of the lucky ones — studying at Georgetown University, a great institution on the cusp of the Ivy League and a pipeline into Wall Street. It has a track record of producing impressive graduates, including the owner of the Wizards and Capitals, noted Shark Tank investor Chris Sacca, former President Bill Clinton, countless well-known politicians, and many other people I'd love to know — let alone one day be.*

*Yet, I felt unfulfilled.*

*I had no idea what my dinner guest would say. She was studying at Harvard. If I was fortunate, she was damn near blessed. I mean, talk about being handed the golden keys to the world.*

*She finished the noodle in her mouth and pulled her napkin off her lap to dab her mouth and chin. Then she rested the napkin back on her lap and put her hands on the table.*

*"Good question."*

**

A quick Google search of some of the most successful leaders in the startup world yields a list that reads like a "Who's Who" of dropouts:

- **Michael Dell**, Dell founder, dropped out at 19

- **Steve Jobs**, Apple founder, dropped out at 19
- **Julian Assange**, Wikileaks founder, dropped out at 19
- **Bill Gates**, Microsoft founder, dropped out at 20
- **Evan Williams**, Twitter co-founder, dropped out at 20
- **Mark Zuckerberg**, Facebook founder, dropped out at 20
- **Larry Ellison**, Oracle founder, dropped out at 20
- **Jan Koum**, WhatsApp founder, dropped out at 21
- **Travis Kalanick**, Uber founder, dropped out at 21
- **John Mackey**, Whole Foods founder, dropped out at 22
- **Richard Branson**, Virgin Group founder, dropped out of high school at 15
- **Daniel Ek**, Spotify founder, dropped out of a university in Sweden

So no, I'm not alone. My friends and I routinely discuss our career goals and constantly question whether or not the "traditional" education system actually works for our generation.

The crazy thing is that, despite the reality that more and more entrepreneurial-minded students like me are considering "dropping out," it is rarely discussed in the entrepreneurial world. PayPal co-founder and noted investor Peter Thiel caused quite the stir when he announced that his Thiel Fellowship would pay bright high school graduates *not* to go to school and instead spend a two years working on whatever inspired them. Thiel's message of a failed educational system met critiques of privilege and hypocrisy, as Thiel himself was a beneficiary of "the system" as a graduate of a prestigious law school.

However, there is data to support Thiel's premise. United States Secretary of Education William J. Bennett rated the lifetime return on investment for several major colleges and universities. It turns out that high-performing high school seniors would actually lose potential earning power if they went to certain colleges, rather than going straight into the workforce after graduation. It is becoming more and more clear that college education alone does not necessarily prepare most students for this new economy.

And here I am, stuck between two worlds.

**

*It was somewhat ironic that we were sitting at a Chinese restaurant less than a mile from the White House, where my friend was interning for the semester. Like many other remarkable students that I am fortunate to know, she had high grades, impressive work experience, and leadership experiences on campus. Also, she started a company during her senior year.*

*"My classes aren't that great or meaningful," she offered. "Even worse, I feel like I'm not getting much value out of classes — especially given the cost we pay every year for school. College could be so much better."*

*"Maybe my expectations are out of whack," I responded. "But the quality of what I'm learning is way below my expectations. Most content I've learned isn't practical, useful, or intellectually stimulating."*

*We both identified ourselves as "entrepreneurial." Even if we weren't actively starting companies, we had started student organizations, and we wanted to proactively lead our lives, instead of unconsciously going with the flow.*

*And we both agreed that there seemed to be a good number of people like us.*

\*\*

Seventy percent of millennials want to start a company one day, according to a recent survey.[1]

While we may not quite know what type of company or when, there's a vast number of us who are no longer enthusiastic about the opportunities we see on the "traditional corporate" path. Consequently, entrepreneurs became our new inspiration. And we hope to join them in their adventures someday. My friend and I are fairly representative case studies of our generation: highly involved, engaged, and inspired students, yet dissatisfied with the way we're being prepared for our futures.

What sets us apart is not that we want more. It's that we are *hungry* for more. If you are like us — if you are willing to take action to make things better — this sets you apart, too. We do not want to waste four precious years in college by going with the flow, getting good grades, and doing club activities just for the sake of it. We want to be entrepreneurs — movers and shakers. Our college classes don't seem to provide us the knowledge and skills we crave. Instead of complaining about it, we are creating an epic college experience that prepares us for an entrepreneurial journey.

Not all students who identify as entrepreneurial are like us. There are other students whose motivations are different. Some are anxious about money. Some see opportunities outside the college "box." This book also will be valuable for any students who are interested in starting a business, working for a startup, creating something meaningful, or bringing about positive change.

**

This book was written for me.

My friends probably would describe me as "unique" in the way I approach my college experience. While most of them are running after fancy jobs on Wall Street, in consulting companies, or at Fortune 500 companies, I've never been interested in any of that.

I'm an entrepreneur. I don't exactly know how that'll play out for my career. However, I know I get irritated when I think of the usual, predictable career path — following instructions and being valued by hours worked instead of the outcome created. I love creating new things or taking the initiative to improve current systems, instead of playing within the rules of the system.

Like most students, I ditch classes sometimes. Unlike most, I ditched classes to listen to successful entrepreneurs speak, attend the live stream of TechCrunch Disrupt, or participate in self-development events featuring **people who have created the outcomes in their own lives that I want to see in mine.**

My college experience was far from normal, and that's why — with some regularity — I contemplated dropping out.

I wanted to write a book that would examine how my role models successfully combined college with their entrepreneurial aspirations. However, most of them took a road less traveled, and their path was to drop out like Zuckerberg, Jobs, or Gates.

But is that the right path for me or those like me?

Is there another way? A way to have my cake and eat it too? A way to retain the value of a college degree but build a base for my future entrepreneurial ventures?

My college experience started differently than many of my peers. In some ways, that was because I was searching for my own path and had to create it without someone to guide me.

- During my first two years in college, I co-founded two student organizations with visions and missions that inspired me.
- I wanted to help after the earthquake hit Nepal. Along with my good friend at Georgetown, who used to live in Nepal, we raised funds, organized a local team, and carried out the project of rebuilding a rural school for 500 students.
- I went to events where extraordinary people were speaking at. And I was fortunate enough to speak with, meet, or listen to:
  - Former U.S. President, Bill Clinton
  - Prime Minister of Malaysia, Najib Razak
  - Noted investor, Warren Buffett
  - Microsoft Founder, Bill Gates
  - PayPal Co-founder and respected Venture Capitalist, Peter Thiel
  - CEO of General Electric, Jeff Immelt
  - CEO of Morgan Stanley, James Gorman
  - Owner of The Washington Wizards and former President of AOL, Ted Leonsis
  - Renowned Peak Performance Strategist, Tony Robbins

- Social Media Expert, Gary Vaynerchuk
- Former White House Press Secretary, Jay Carney
- Former Secretary of Commerce, Carlos M. Gutierrez

- In an average semester, I flew out to attend two self-development seminars and read at least ten personal development books to expand my horizons. (Some seminars unfortunately overlapped with my exam schedules, but we will save these stories for later.)

- Lest you think I just "phoned it in" on the academic front: while I'm definitely not the valedictorian, I made sure my parents smiled when they saw my name on Dean's List every semester.

**

Here's the thing:

**I was not going to drop out of college.** I wanted to maximize my college experience to best prepare myself for an entrepreneurial journey and a good life. Therefore, I embarked on this journey of discovering what I should think about, learn, and do in my free time to help achieve that.

After that discussion over Chinese noodles with my close friend and some quick research, I realized it was difficult to find the answers I was looking for. I would have to blaze the trail myself.

This book catalogs my journey of discovery: a bit like a journal, a scrapbook, and a counseling session rolled into one. I've written about what I spent over five years learning, uncovering, and collecting — and consolidated it to share with others who are ready to take charge of their own lives and do things differently.

This is my journey of seeking answers from successful entrepreneurs because I believe, as Tony Robbins says, "Success leaves clues." What would they have done in college knowing what they know today? I identified some of the most iconic entrepreneurs of our time such as Mark Zuckerberg, Richard Branson, Bill Gates, and Elon Musk. And I researched their paths to success, as well as the advice they have for young people. I also conducted personal interviews with successful entrepreneurs, including the co-founder of Honest Tea, the founder of *Foundr Magazine*, the co-founder of MasterClass, and several others at cool companies. Through these interviews, themes and patterns appeared quickly. It became fun at the end to correctly predict the answers these experts would give to certain questions.

At the onset of my work, I hoped that I would identify some patterns and common answers that would be applicable to my life and the lives of other students. I was excited to find a high number of interesting patterns and tools that I am excited to share with you in this book.

While this started as a nagging issue and developed into a conversation with trusted friends who were also craving more from college, it grew into a quest. I am not dropping out, and regardless of which of the paths you choose, I hope you are inspired to own your experience in college and your life.

**

I invite you to embrace the entrepreneurial spirit, but this does not mean you have to start a business. "Entrepreneur" has a broader meaning:

- Entrepreneurs choose to take full control of their lives by assuming the risks, responsibility, and accountability associated with their decisions. They take complete ownership of their lives and life circumstances.
- Entrepreneurs think differently and purposefully. They do not just follow crowds or rules. Instead, they decide consciously what they want and go after it.
- Entrepreneurs work harder than anyone else to make their visions a reality.
- Entrepreneurs defy the status quo by constantly thinking about ways to make things better. More importantly, they consistently initiate new and better processes and products.
- Entrepreneurs are resourceful, and they make the most of that is available to them.

This book is not a manual that teaches you how to start a company step-by-step. You won't find tips and tricks about how to generate product ideas, conduct customer interviews, or create a viable product. **What you will find are the start-up mindsets and skill sets that you can use to prepare yourself for an entrepreneurial journey and to maximize your college experience.**

Are you...

- Ready to consciously take charge of your college experience and create something epic and rewarding?
- Ready to explore the journey of entrepreneurship?
- Ready to take the path less traveled?
- If your answer is yes, then you must be a kindred spirit, and I am more than excited to have you join this journey of discovery and learning with me.

Here's to the crazy ones.

— ANTONIA LIU

# HOW TO HACK
# THIS BOOK

———

Treat this book like a buffet. Below are some suggestions to help you get the most out of it:

## IDENTIFY WHAT YOU WANT OUT OF THIS BOOK

Having clear outcomes is a powerful yet often overlooked hack to creating great results. This entire book is about how to live your life and college experience more deliberately. Let's start this habit right here. **Write down the five questions you want this book to answer for you.** Then go look for the answers.

Treat each chapter as an independent, powerful hack.

Do not let the pressure of needing to finish this book prevent you from starting. Even though some chapters are connected, most of them stand on their own. Just read the ones that grab your attention and, more importantly, take action. No one chapter can turn you into a millionaire entrepreneur or Rhodes Scholar, but each chapter has the power to impact your entrepreneurial journey if executed well.

## ONLY USE THE STRUCTURE AS A GUIDE

The structure of the book is made up of three main sections (what to think about, what to learn, and what to do) and three subgroups under each section (as a person, as a student, as an entrepreneur). This structure is put in place to help you better understand this book. Many chapters are interconnected and can fall into different sections and groups. Do not let the structure limit you. Jump into any chapters that interest you.

## SKIP LIBERALLY

Skip anything that doesn't grab your attention. Let this book be fun to read and a buffet to choose from. Again, you do not have to read and follow all forty hacks. Keep your outcome in mind, and select the hacks that best serve you.

## TAKE ACTION!

Knowledge is not power. Knowledge is only potential power. Nothing will happen unless you take action. Make sure you check off the *Action Checklist* at the end of each chapter. Implementing three chapters would be more effective than reading thirty chapters.

## PART 1

# WHAT TO THINK ABOUT

# CHAPTER 1

# WHY DO YOU DESERVE IT?

———

*"To get what you want, you have to deserve what you want. The world is not yet a crazy enough place to reward a whole bunch of undeserving people."*

— CHARLIE MUNGER

*"Life is about creating yourself."*

— ANONYMOUS

I want to open the first chapter with one of the most profound and helpful exercises I have encountered.

A college student asked Buffett this question when he was speaking to a room full of students, "Mr. Warren Buffett, can you give us some advice on how to be successful like you?"

Buffett responded with a powerful thought experiment.

"I'm giving you an offer. You can pick any of your classmates, and you will get 10% of their earnings for the rest of your life. What goes through your mind? (You can't pick the one with the richest father, it won't count.) Think about who you would pick and why.

"You probably won't pick the one who has the highest grade in the class. Interesting enough, it all comes down to a list of qualities that are self-made. It's not about how tall you are, how far you can kick a football, or the best-looking person. It's a list of qualities, such as integrity, honesty, willingness to do more than your share, generosity, and more. These are all self-selected, meaning anyone can cultivate those traits. Also, on the other side, think of the person you think will do the worst and why. This is way more fun."

"The good news is these qualities can be acquired and taken out. They are not ordained. Look at the list of good qualities. Identify which ones you do not have yet, and cultivate the qualities you desire deliberately. Ben Franklin did this, and my old boss Ben Graham did this, in their early years. Ben Graham asked himself who he admired and for what reasons. **He decided what kind of person he wanted to be**

**and took action**. This is something achievable by everyone in this room."

Buffett's words hit me hard. I imagine a mic drop at the end of his talk. What a great hack on success!

Tony Robbins, a renowned peak performance strategist, says that the goal is not to reach the goal because reaching the goal will only bring you happiness for a very short period of time. The real goal is to become the person who can reach the goal. Why? Because no one can take away who we are. And the joy we get from improving ourselves does not fade away.

After working and interacting with millions of people around the world, Tony identifies the strongest force in human psychology is the need to stay consistent with one's identity. He uses a thermostat as an analogy for our identity. If the temperature is set at 70 degrees, and the room temperature drops to 65 the thermostat will kick in and say, "Get up there, you know you are better than this." However, the interesting thing is that the same effect happens on the other side as well. If the set temperature is 70 degrees, and things go really well while you may experience some success, raising the temperature up to 80 degrees. In this case, your internal thermostat will kick in and cool down the situation by saying, "Who do you think you are? You aren't worthy! Stop being an 80-degree person! Remember? You are a 70-degree person!"

It is a simple analogy, but it also applies to all the labels we put on ourselves. **What labels or descriptions do you attach to yourself?** Did you actually choose those labels and identities? Most of us adopt the beliefs and personalities that our families gave us. From a very young age, we start to attach labels to ourselves: smart, outgoing, shy, hardworking, lazy, and many more. **The good news is you can change many of these labels because your pattern of behavior is not who you ARE. At any moment, you have the power to make a decision and change.** You can work two extra hours and just that quickly, you've reversed your pattern of laziness. You can force yourself to talk to one stranger every day to stop labeling yourself as shy. It's all up to you.

However, you can't be who you want to be without knowing who you want to be first!

## ACTION CHECKLIST

☐ Write down 10 characteristics of people you admire.

☐ Write down 5-10 characteristics or labels you find on yourself.

☐ Who do you want to become? Write down 10 characteristics in the order of importance.

☐ Define each characteristic with 1-3 actions.

☐ Create a plan to gain those characteristics by practicing them.

CHAPTER 2

# WHAT IF YOU COULD HAVE ANYTHING?

———

*When you want something, the whole universe conspires to make it happen.*

— PAULO COELHO

*People are not lazy. They just do not have goals that inspire them.*

— TONY ROBBINS

Here is a story that shifted my mind and touched my heart.

"There is an old couple who have been living a thrifty life. One of their dreams was to go on a cruise to The Caribbean. They saved money for ten years for this one-week dream cruise trip that will take them to see all the most beautiful parts of the Caribbean. They were very excited, but they were still concerned about saving money, so they decided to pack food for the entire trip. The food they packed included the baloney sandwiches they normally ate for lunch, pretzels, chips, and water. During the trip, they enjoyed the views and couldn't help but look at all the amazing food and fancy wines others were enjoying. Yet, they still returned to their room during every meal time to eat the boring food they packed. On the last day, they finally decided that they had to treat themselves once before the trip is over. They went to the restaurant, ordered their favorite dishes, and enjoyed a great meal. After eating, the husband asked for the check. The waiter looked at them with confusion. What check? This is an all-inclusive cruise trip. Where have you guys been eating for the past six days? The waiter asked. The old couple looked at each other and did not speak a word."

If life was an all-you-can-eat buffet, what do want to enjoy? Have you been putting restraints on yourself about what you can't have? **Right now, write down a list of the most important things you want in life.** Include whatever comes to mind, and do not allow questions stop you (don't ask "How can I make this happen?"). For our *biocomputers* to create a result, we need to be very specific. For example, instead of "a new car," you should write the brand, color, year, and model that you want. As you create your list, some of the things you write down will be things you've thought about for years. Some will be things you've never consciously formulated before. Once you have chosen your destination, there are many ways to get there.

**The key is to know where you want to go first.** When I do this, I am always surprised to see how little focus I have been putting on what I wanted. Living life without focusing on what I want is like wandering in a forest and hoping to get somewhere. I have noticed that whenever I redirect my focus back on the important things I want, my thinking and behavior shift automatically. It's like how GPS readjusts when veering from the suggested route; when a goal is set, your thinking adjusts automatically.

**The reason most people fail to live a meaningful, enjoyable, and exciting life is that they never consider what they want in a clear and specific way.** If they have goals, they may not believe they can achieve those goals, and, consequently, their actions and results are predictably ineffective.

How sad is it to settle for a mediocre life simply because you did not dream big enough? **You are constrained by your limited beliefs about who you are, what you can do, and what you can have.** Granted, it is hard to dream big and ask for all that you want from life because most people do not do this. Most people are not necessarily cynical, pessimistic, or skeptical. They are just afraid of being disappointed, again.

This is not just positive thinking fluff! **It is a call to be one of the few people who are happy, healthy, wealthy, *and* passionate about work.** All you need to do is study the techniques and patterns of the great ones. As Tony Robbins says, "Success leaves clues." If you want to be healthy, study people who are in great shape. If you want to make a lot of money, study the stories and advice from millionaires. If you want to have good grades, study what traits straight-A students have in common. **If you want a badass life, study the life and characteristics of people who are both kicking butt and enjoying the ride.**

I will share two models that helped me to think about what I want from life.

The first one is developed by Tony Robbins, and he calls it "Areas of Continuous Improvements." The reason is that these are seven areas of life that he believes are the most important. If you do not consciously improve them, they will weaken and your life will be negatively impacted. These seven areas are health & vitality, mind & meaning, love & relationships, productivity & performance, career & business, wealth & lifestyle, celebration & contribution. Rate yourself for each area on a scale of 1-10, and then put down the number for each area that you want to excel in.[1]

A second framework is from Michael Hyatt, the author of a life-planning book *Living Forward: A Proven Plan to Stop*

*Drifting and Get the Life You Want.* Start by thinking of all of the various components that make up your life. Most people can organize their lives into seven to twelve distinct areas. We call these Life Accounts. Over his many years of teaching, Hyatt found the following to be the nine most common Life Accounts. Note that the Life Accounts diagram is made up of three concentric circles emanating from the center — you.[2]

**The Circle of Being.** The innermost ring is a collection of activities focused solely on you in relation to yourself. It includes your spiritual, intellectual, and physical accounts.

**The Circle of Relating.** The second ring is a collection of activities centered on you in relation to others: your marital, parental, and social accounts (e.g., friendships, church or synagogue, book club, and so on).

**The Circle of Doing.** The third ring is a collection of activities dealing with you in relation to your output: your vocation (job), avocation (hobbies), and financial accounts.

This is a great model to help you recognize that your life is more than just one account. It is more than work. It is more than marriage. It is more than money. It is an interrelated collection of interests, responsibilities, dreams, and activities. People create different life accounts. For example, Jerry has nine: Self, Marriage, Kids, Parents and Siblings, Friends,

Career Finances, Creating, and Pets. Hannah has eight: Faith, Self-care, Family, Extended Family, Finances, Work, Teaching, Adventure. My accounts would be: Health & Vitality, Emotions, Mission & Career, School, Family, Friends, Time, Legacy.

As you think through your own list, here are four considerations:

- Your Life Accounts are unique to you.
- Your Life Accounts can be named whatever you want.
- Your Life Accounts are interrelated.
- Your Life Accounts will change over time.[3]

So, now let's use a broad brush to paint a picture of what you want.

## ACTION CHECKLIST

☐ Write down 5 things you desire the most in life

☐ What would you do if you knew you couldn't fail? Add those to your list!

☐ Identify 7-10 most important areas (life accounts) of your life.

☐ What do you want from each area? Identify the outcome or goal in each area.

☐ Create visualizations for yourself.

☐ What is the ideal health, school, career, family look like to you?

CHAPTER 3

# WHAT DO YOU LOVE?

———

*"You really need to like what you are doing. If you don't, life is too short."*

— ELON MUSK

*"Your work is going to fill a large part of your life, and the only way to be truly satisfied is to do what you believe is great work. And the only way to do great work is to love what you do. If you haven't found it yet, keep looking. Don't settle."*

— STEVE JOBS

"It was nearly impossible for me to keep up in school due to my dyslexia, so I left at 16 to start a magazine." Richard Branson says that he found his passion and focus in creating the magazine — it even kept him up all night at times. "It also helped me to stay positive during stressful times and to tackle the challenges that arose as our team grew *Student* into a better magazine."[1]

Seth Goldman, co-founder of Honest Tea, told me that the most important thing for college students to think about is identifying and developing interests. "You will always be a more effective entrepreneur when you are doing something you care about," according to Seth. Do not worry if your passion does not seem to have a connection with the business world. Seth was and still is passionate about running, so he was always interested in solving problems for runners. As an avid runner, Seth is often thirsty, but he couldn't find healthy and flavorful beverages in the market. And this led him to co-found a company that offers a healthier beverage, organic tea with clean ingredients. Nineteen years later, Honest Tea has sold more than one billion bottles and can be found in more than 200,000 stores around the world.

You have probably heard of "follow your passion" millions of times. It is true that following your passion is important and beneficial. **But how do you know what your passion *is*?**

Here are some clues:

## TRACK WHAT LIGHTS YOU UP

The next time you feel energized, excited, happy, strong, fully alive, or that time is flying — write it down!

## GO BACK TO YOUR CHILDHOOD

"Have you seen a kid who is not passionate or excited? No! So, my advice to people is to recall what you loved and were passionate about when you were young." Bill Carmody, the founder of a digital advertising agency, shared his advice with me passionately.

## TRY LOTS OF THINGS

It's hard to know if you like something or not if you haven't done it before, right? As simple as it sounds, I find that most students I know are not trying out a variety of work experiences to help them identify their passions. Liz, the co-founder of WayUP (a top online platform that connects students with employers), believes that working experience is the best way to identify one's passion. Liz tried many internships in different industries during her school years and summers to help her identify what she loves to do. She was a politics and government major because she thought that's what she wanted to do. However, after experiencing a political career firsthand with her internship, she realized that politics wasn't for her. She had a similar experience with finance after spending a summer doing a private equity internship with one of the biggest financial firms in the world. On the other hand, she did not realize that she liked marketing until she tried a marketing internship at Google. Liz was happy to find her passion through internships instead of through real jobs after graduation.

Nathan Chan, the founder of *Foundr Magazine*, told me that a significant contributor to his success is he did not give up his quest to find the work he loved. He did not give up. After interviewing some of the iconic entrepreneurs of our time, Nathan also saw this pattern in many other entrepreneurs. They tried many different work and jobs until they found what they loved to do. The key is to be willing to try different things, and refuse to settle until you find something that you are excited about.

Look for the motivation behind your favorite activities.

Your passion may not necessarily be the activities themselves — but they will have something in common. Look into them and behind them for shared motivation and emotions until you find what playwrights call a character's throughline: the essence of what you're good at and what drives you.

For example, Steve Jobs was not passionate about computers per se, any more than he was passionate about calligraphy or Japanese gardening. He was passionate about simplicity, so he made it his obsession and his art. He introduced it to an industry that, as far as it was concerned, was doing just fine without it. Simplicity drove the Apple identity: the strategy, the products, the marketing and branding, and the presentations. Simplicity enabled a computer company to connect with mass culture on a deep, emotional level. Jobs brought his love of simplicity home just as fiercely: the complications of a couch, for example his living room didn't require one.[2]

## ACTION CHECKLIST

☐ Start a list (on your phone or in a journal) of what "lights you up."
☐ Remember what you loved as a child.
☐ Identify at least 3 activities that you love.
☐ Make a list of at least 5 new things you'd like to try.
☐ Identify 3 passions you have and think about what those have in common.

# CHAPTER 4

# ARE YOU "SO GOOD THAT THEY CAN'T IGNORE YOU"?

—

*"Telling someone to follow their passion — from an entrepreneur's point of view — is disastrous. That advice has probably resulted in more failed businesses than all the recessions combined... because that's not how the vast majority of people end up owning successful businesses."*

— CAL NEWPORT

*"Passion is not something you follow. Passion is something that will follow you as you put in the hard work to become valuable to the world."*

— CAL NEWPORT

The world doesn't owe you happiness. Your boss has no reason to let you choose your own projects, or spend one week out of every four writing a novel at your beach house. If you are an entrepreneur, the market has no reason to let your company make millions of dollars a year or give you the free time or flexibility you want. These rewards are valuable and rare. Cal Newport, author of *So Good They Can't Ignore You: Why Skills Trump Passion in the Search for Work You Love*, believes that **to earn these rewards, you must accumulate your own career capital by mastering skills that are equally rare and valuable.**[1]

Almost every entrepreneur I interviewed told me that students need to be REALLY good at something. So, if you are not REALLY good at something relevant to your goal, ask yourself why you would succeed versus the other millions of people trying to do the same.

Based on my observations, the importance of skills is over-looked by most people. Very few students think about acquiring important and marketable skills that can help them in any career they choose. Instead, they just take classes that everyone else is taking and hope things will work out. It is very clear that the world is putting less and less value on degrees. Many students from prestigious schools and even MBA programs have a hard time finding jobs. The reason is simple: they do not have the skills that will add value to the companies that are hiring.

Cal Newport's book attracted a lot of attention and controversy around the topic of passion. (Yes, I know that I said to find your passion in the last chapter.) The bad news is that passion is not the whole picture. The good news is that if you cannot find a "soul-calling" passion, you do not need to worry. **Of course, it is always nice to do something you love doing, but if you haven't found it, you do not need to stress out because Cal discovered that most people develop a professional passion through their work.** Instead of worrying about pursuing passion, Cal believes that people should focus on developing one or multiple valuable skills and become "so good they cannot ignore you."[2]

Here's why:

- **Career Passions Are Rare.** People rarely have career passions that are hobbies or interests. If you don't get paid enough for your passion, it's not a career passion.
- **Passion Takes Time.** According to research, what is the strongest predictor of a person seeing their work as a calling? The number of years spent on the job. Why? The more experience you have, the better your skills and the deeper your relationships to the field. Where business success is concerned, passion is almost always the result of time and effort. It's not a prerequisite.
- **Passion Is a Side Effect of Mastery.** The satisfaction of achieving one level of success spurs you on to gain the skills to reach the next level, and the next, and the next. And one day you wake

up feeling incredibly fulfilled. "The satisfaction of improving is deeply satisfying," Cal says. **"The process of becoming really good at something valuable is a fulfilling and satisfying process in itself...and is the foundation for a great entrepreneurial career."**

- **Working Right Trumps Finding the Right Work.** Want to love what you do? First, pick something interesting and financially viable. Then, work hard: improve your skills, whether at managing, selling, creating, implementing — whatever skills your business requires. Use the satisfaction and fulfillment of small victories as motivation to keep working hard.

What are you better at than everyone else? According to iconic entrepreneur and investor Peter Thiel, "the most important factor for a startup to grasp" is to be doing one thing uniquely well, better than anybody else in the world." Thiel told CNN Money, "Technology is a fundamentally global business and the really great technology companies are doing something significantly better than anybody else in the world. You want to be in that sort of business."[3]

Every company needs a core competitive advantage, and the same thing goes for a person. If we follow the famous axiom that it takes 10,000 hours to master something, what skill would you like to master? What do you want to be better at than everyone else? What do you want to be so good at that they cannot ignore you?

I know 10,000 hours sounds crazy, maybe even impossible, to achieve. But guess what? If you had a solid plan and direction in freshman year and spent class time and non-class time crafting that skill, you would have 10,000 hours in before you graduate year and be a master of the skill you chose. And yes, it's possible because you do have a lot of free time in college. **By the way, it might not take 10,000 hours if you hack a skill by studying the best in the field.**

## ACTION CHECKLIST

☐ Identify 3 skills you want to develop.

☐ Choose the most important skill you are excited to master.

☐ Develop a plan for learning to master the skill for the first 100 hours. Block out time in your calendar to make sure it happens.

☐ Take action now and start learning, time is ticking.

# CHAPTER 5

# WHAT IS YOUR COMPETITIVE ADVANTAGE?

---

*"Anything you can do I can do better. I can do anything better than you."*

— LYRICS FROM "ANYTHING YOU CAN DO"

BY IRVING BERLIN

Reid Hoffman, co-founder of LinkedIn, wrote *Startup of You: Adapt to the Future, Invest in Yourself, and Transform Your Career*. The first chapter of the book is dedicated to competitive advantage. It is easy to see how important Reid thinks this point is, and I agree with him. Whether you are an entrepreneur or not, you need a way to stand out from the crowd.

This chapter features Reid Hoffman's insights on identifying and building your competitive advantage.

A billboard on 101 Highway in the Bay Area in 2009 put it bluntly: "1,000,000 people overseas can do your job. What makes you so special?" While one million might be an exaggeration, what's not an exaggeration is many people can do and want to have your dream job. For anything desirable, there's competition: a ticket to a championship game, an attractive life partner, or admission to a good college. **Being better than the competition is essential to an entrepreneur's survival.**

In every sector, multiple companies compete for a single customer's dollar. The world is loud and messy; customers don't have time to parse minute differences. Products must be massively different to command market share. As Do Something CEO Nancy Lublin says, the new product should be **"first, only, faster, better, or cheaper."** Successful entrepreneurs build and brand products that are differentiated from the competition. They are able to finish the sentence, "Our customers buy from us and not that other company because…" For example, Zappos.com, the online shoe retailer founded in 1999, has "insanely good customer service."[1]

Of course, you are different from an online shoe store, but you are selling your brainpower, your skills, and your energy in the face of massive competition. If you want to chart a course that differentiates you from other professionals in the marketplace, the first step is being able to complete the sentence, "A company hires me over other professionals because...." How are you "first, only, faster, better, or cheaper" than other people who want to do what you're doing in the world? What are you offering that's hard to come by? What are you offering that's both rare and valuable?

**You don't need to be better or faster or cheaper than everyone, contrary to the song at the beginning of the chapter.** Companies don't compete in every product category or offer every conceivable service. In other words, don't try to be the greatest marketing executive in the world; try to be the greatest marketing executive of small-to-midsize companies that compete in the restaurant industry.

What we explain in this chapter is how to determine the local niche in which you can develop a competitive advantage. **Competitive advantage underpins all career strategy.** It helps answer the classic question, "What should I be doing with my life?" It helps you decide which opportunities to pursue. It guides you in how you should be investing in yourself. **Because all of these things change, assessing and evaluating your competitive advantage is a lifelong process, not something you do once.** It's done by understanding three dynamic puzzle pieces that fit together in different ways at different times.[2]

## HOW TO IDENTIFY (AND DEVELOP) YOUR COMPETITIVE ADVANTAGE[3]

### 1. ASSETS

Before dreaming about the future or making plans, you need to articulate what you already have going for you — as entrepreneurs do. The most brilliant business idea is often the one that builds on the founders' existing assets in the most brilliant way. For example, Larry Page and Sergey Brin started Google Page when they were in a computer science doctoral program. Their business goals emerged from their strengths, interests, and network of contacts.

**You have two types of career assets to keep track of: soft and hard.** Soft assets are things you can't trade directly for money. They're the intangible contributors to career success: the knowledge and experience; professional connections and the trust you've built up with them; skills you've mastered; your reputation and personal brand; your strengths (things that come easily to you). Hard assets are what you'd typically list on a balance sheet: the cash in your wallet; the stocks you own; physical possessions like your desk and laptop. They matter because when you have an economic cushion, you can more aggressively make moves that entail downside financial risk.

Your asset mix is not fixed. You can strengthen it by investing in yourself — that's what this book is about. If you think you lack certain assets that would make you more competitive, don't use it as an excuse. Start developing them.

## 2. ASPIRATIONS AND VALUES

Aspirations include your deepest wishes, ideas, goals, and vision of the future. This piece of the puzzle includes your core values, or what's important to you in life, be it knowledge, autonomy, money, integrity, power, and so on. You may not be able to achieve all your aspirations or build a life that incorporates all your values, but anchoring yourself by your values provides the soft assets of integrity and continuity.

Aspirations and values are both important pieces of your career competitive advantage simply because, when you're doing work you care about, you are able to work harder and better.

Jack Dorsey is co-founder and executive chairman of Twitter and co-founder and CEO of Square, a mobile credit card payments start-up. He's known in Silicon Valley as a product visionary who prizes design, and his inspirations vary widely — from Steve Jobs to the Golden Gate Bridge. Both his companies have grown to towering heights, while keeping Jack's values and priorities intact. Twitter is still minimalistic and clean; the Square device is still elegant. His aspiration to make complex things simple and his value of design are part of the reason his companies have been so successful:

they clarify product priorities, ensure a consistent customer experience, and make it easier to recruit employees who are attracted to similar ideas.

## 3. MARKET REALITIES

Smart entrepreneurs know a product won't make money if customers don't want or need it, regardless of how slick its form and function (think of the Segway). Likewise, your skills, experiences, and other soft assets — no matter how special you think they are — won't give you an edge unless they meet customer needs. In short, will people pay you for what you offer? It's often said that entrepreneurs are dreamers. True. But good entrepreneurs are also firmly grounded in opportunities of what is possible right now. Specifically, entrepreneurs spend vast amounts of energy trying to figure out what customers will pay for.

## FIT THE PIECES TOGETHER

A good career plan accounts for the interplay of the three pieces — your assets, aspirations, and the market realities. **The pieces need to fit together.** Developing a key skill, for example, doesn't automatically give you a competitive edge. Just because you're good at something (assets) that you're really passionate about (aspirations) doesn't necessarily mean someone will pay you to do it (market realities). After all, what if someone else can do the same thing for lower pay or do it more reliably? Or what if there's no demand for the skill to begin with? Not a very useful competitive advantage. Following your passions also doesn't automatically lead to a career flourishing. What if you're passionate but not competent, relative to others? Finally, being a slave to market realities isn't sustainable.[4]

## ACTION CHECKLIST

- ☐ Identify and create your competitive advantages. Fill in the blanks to find yours: : "Because of my _____ [skill/experience/strength], I can do _____ [type of work] better than _____ [specific types of other people in the industry]."
- ☐ Identify 3 people who are striving toward aspirations similar to your own. Use them as benchmarks. What are their differentiators? How did they get to where they are? Bookmark their LinkedIn profiles, subscribe to their blogs and tweets. Track their professional evolution and take inspiration and insight from their journeys.
- ☐ Write down some of your key assets in the context of a market reality. BAD: I excel at public speaking. GOOD: I excel at public speaking on engineering topics, relative to how good most engineers are at public speaking.

# CHAPTER 6

# 20 QUESTIONS TO "KNOW THYSELF"

___

*"Judge a man by his questions rather than his answers."*

— PIERRE-MARC-GASTON

*"Successful people ask better questions, so they get better answers."*

— TONY ROBBINS

## KNOW YOURSELF

The first step to maximize any system is to get to know the system. Same applies to people. Gary Vaynerchuk, the founder of VaynerMedia, claim that self-awareness is your most important attribute. This charismatic entrepreneur's message is to know your shortcomings and strive to become more conscious of who you really are. I agree with him.

These self-awareness questions came from the input of my good friend Molham Krayem who started his first company at Georgetown University. Molham is a consultant at Bain, contributor to Forbes Middle East, and curious lifelong learner. He plans on going back to being a founder in a few years. Here are the ten great questions worth pondering:

1. Am I everything I could be/want to be? Where's the discrepancy between my current self and my ideal self? What's missing? (Look at the lists you've created and identify gaps; this is what you need to target and where you need to grow.)

2. What are my life's three most significant and defining stories? How can I best craft these stories to share with others? Think about how could tell your history with three good stories.

3. Why do I share what I share on social media? To educate, to entertain, to inform? Is it of any value to others?

4. If I had a billion dollars in the bank, what would I do? Don't think about what you would buy/spend money on; rather, consider you would spend your time if you didn't have to worry about money? That is, what are you naturally happy doing?

5. If I were to look at my schedule and how I'm spending my time, would it reflect my values, purpose, and ambitions? If not, why? And, if not, how can I more consciously spend my time.

6. What's one thing I can do that will dramatically change my life

for the better? What will "change the game?" What would make my life (this day, this week, this class, etc.) a "ten"?

7. How do I perceive myself? Describe yourself in a short paragraph.

8. What am I doing that is secretly a distraction? The things that I'm only half-a**ing and are — in the grand scheme of things (and my happiness) — unnecessary? What are the things that I need to eliminate from my schedule to make room for what's necessary?

9. What do I want people to say at my funeral?

10. What makes me come alive? (For more details, refer to the "What Do You Love" chapter.)

## 10 QUESTIONS TO EXPAND YOUR THINKING

Tim Ferriss said, "World-class performers don't have super-powers. The rules they've crafted for themselves to allow the bending of reality to such an extent that it may seem that way, but they've learned how to do this, and so can you." These "rules" are often uncommon habits and bigger questions. In a surprising number of cases, the power is in the absurd. The more absurd, the more "impossible" the question, the more profound the answers.

Take, for instance, a question that serial billionaire Peter Thiel likes to ask himself and others: "If you have a ten-year plan of how to get [somewhere], you should ask: Why can't you do this in six months?" For purposes of illustration here, I might reword that to: "What might you do to accomplish your ten-year goals in the next six months, if you had a gun against your head?"

Do I expect you to take 10 seconds to ponder this and then magically accomplish 10 years' worth of dreams in the next few months? No. However, I **expect that this question will productively break open your mind, like a butterfly shattering a chrysalis to emerge with new capabilities.**

The "normal" systems you have in place, the social rules you've forced upon yourself, the standard frameworks — they don't work when answering a question like this. You are forced to shed artificial constraints, like shedding a skin, to realize that you had the ability to renegotiate your reality all along. It just takes practice."[1]

1.  What would I do if I couldn't fail?
2.  Why couldn't I achieve my ten-year goal in the next six months?
3.  What is something I believe in that most people disagree with me about?
4.  What if life always happens *for* me, not *to* me?
5.  What are the worst things that could happen? Could I get back here?
6.  If I could only work five hours per week on studying (or your business), what would I do?
7.  What would this look like if it were easy?

8. How can I add more value to people around me (or your customers) than anyone else?
9. How hard would I try if I knew I would be successful?
10. How can I be a blessing to people around me?

CHAPTER 7

# WHAT DO YOU WANT FROM COLLEGE?

———

*"Don't let school interfere with your education."*

— MARK TWAIN

One morning, in the middle of my Junior year, I realized I'd wasted 70% of my time in college. On that morning, I was inspired by a list of audacious goals of my mentor who is a successful entrepreneur and multimillionaire. So I got serious and created a list of clear goals:

1. Have a healthy and energetic body by December 2017.
2. Maintain, expand, and develop my close group of friends and mentors.

3.  Become skilled in practical psychology by 2020, so I can help people to achieve what they want.
4.  Become one of the best marketing strategists in our generation by 2025.
5.  Become a successful entrepreneur with annual revenue of $10 million by the time I turn 30.

It seemed to me that only about 10% of what I learned in my classes (liberal arts, business, and marketing) are relevant to my goals. Yet, I spent the vast majority of my time procrastinating, completing, or stressing over school-related work. As a result, I created excuses for not accomplishing meaningful things like interning, eating well, or connecting with friends or mentors. This artificial and illogical stress also negatively influenced my extra-curricular activities. I have had countless weekends that are spent "working" on school and club projects that I couldn't even remember. All I knew was that I was "too busy" to relax, have fun, or go check out the many amazing national museums two miles from Georgetown. **Of the time I spent in college, only about 30% of my time was spent working toward my goals.** The extra-curricular activities, seminars, time management skills, and cool people I've connected with makeup 20% of time well spent. 10% of my time was learning useful things from classes. The majority of my time was spent doing things that I don't remember. After having this realization, I started laughing. I don't know why, but it is kind of hilarious to realize how silly I have been about my choices and how off base I was.

"Well," I told myself, "the upside is at least I have the awareness now!" As a result, I changed my schedule drastically to allow substantial time every day to learn the best marketing and business materials, to consume information that feeds my mind, to train my body, and to live more consciously. I **took control of my life by changing the present to create the future I want.**

How do you avoid a similar story? Decide what you want and reflect frequently to see if you are on track.

**Identifying what you want to learn is key. Pick classes that are aligned with that.** For every class you take, including the mandatory ones, list out the top three things you want to learn from the course or professor.

**A good way to think about this is if you were to write the syllabus, what exactly you would want to learn.** Do not settle until you actually learn those things. Talk to your professor. Ask questions in class. Dig into the relevant readings. Whatever it takes. Once you've clarified your ideal outcome for each class, your motivation to engage with the material will go through the roof. Even if you do not get any other benefits, your professor will be impressed that you have set goals for your learning. You'll stand out because most students just process whatever material is thrown at them and don't think deeply about it.

Bill Carmody, the founder of Trepoint (a digital marketing agency), had an extraordinary college experience by knowing his outcomes and taking the initiative. I was surprised when I heard this story. Bill went to a small state college in Boston because his dad was on staff at the school so that he could afford the discounted tuition. Bill had a clear outcome for college: he wanted to become a marketing expert by the time he graduated. However, he had a massive problem because the school did not even have a marketing major available. Besides, the school would not do all the work to start a major even if Bill gathered enough interested students. Bill did not give up there. He researched the organization that was in charge of giving accreditation of marketing majors and worked with the school to meet those requirements. In about a year, he was able to help create a marketing major at his college.

He did not stop there. Bill took the initiative to form a team to participate in famous marketing competitions. (Fun Fact: Bill and his team warned Kodak about their decline based on their product design and marketing approach, when Kodak was still one of the most prominent companies in the world. Their opinion was taken lightly but proved to be true.) Further, Bill started a marketing agency with his classmates during school. They leveraged their understanding and expertise in the college student market and tried to convince local businesses to be their clients. They learned mostly through trial and error, but it was a great learning experience for everyone in the company. The startup also used part of its profits to encourage the presence of marketing on campus for interested students by sponsoring activities, including trips to NYC to visit famous advertising agencies. By knowing his outcome and taking the initiative, Bill trained himself to be a marketing expert, and he also established the opportunity for many students to learn marketing.

**I believe you shouldn't let school interfere with your education once you identify exactly what you want to learn.** To illustrate, let me tell you the story of how I skipped the entire final exam period during my first semester in college. Before anyone starts to scream, here's the story. During my freshman year, I badly wanted to go to Tony Robbins' "Date with Destiny" seminar because I had heard many different successful people claim that it is a life-changing experience. I even met one MIT person who told me that he learned more about life in six days at the seminar than in 4 years of MIT. Since I already had some good experiences with Tony, I set my heart on going to the event. **Then I found out that this annual six-day event took up six out of the eight days of my finals period.** What a coincidence. I was very frustrated trying to make this impossible situation work.

After talking to professors and working on my schedule extensively, I ended up in three classes that had final papers and two classes with professors who agreed that I could take my their exams early. In the end, I experienced Date with Destiny, the most powerful, profound, life-changing six days of my life. My story might be a little extreme, but it also shows that **with careful planning, you can do amazing out-of-the-box things that might seem crazy to traditional college students.**

Fun fact: the Date With Destiny I went to is the event where they filmed the documentary "I Am Not Your Guru," which is available on Netflix. You can watch the film and decide if it was worth it for me to go.

## ACTION CHECKLIST

- ☐ Identify the top 5 outcomes you want from college. Create at least 3 goals for this semester. (And for all future semesters)
- ☐ Identify 3 things that apply to your "real-world" goals that you can learn from each of your classes.
- ☐ Communicate your goals to your professors and create a plan to accomplish your outcomes and goals.

## CHAPTER 8

# HOW CAN YOU OPTIMIZE THE NEXT FOUR YEARS?

———

*"If young people do see me as an example (I'm very flattered if they do!), I hope it is as someone who will go out there and live life to the fullest."*

— RICHARD BRANSON

*"Most students are terrible at studying."*

— CAL NEWPORT

**A big part of being an entrepreneur is about being able to optimize resources for a goal.** A pretty safe bet is most college students want good grades, fun, and physical and mental well-being. However, most students are bad at reaching these goals because they have never approached these goals with a plan or strategy. **To be more precise, most students do not think about optimizing their actions to reach the desired result.**

Cal Newport, the author of *How to Win at College* and *How to be a Straight-A student*, shared this with me when I interviewed him:

"**I always tell students to care about how they study and why.** Studying is a skill to be learned and practiced. So you should always be thinking about, questioning, and testing your study techniques. I always tell students this because **most students are terrible at studying.** The techniques students use to read, study, and take notes are terrible. For the most part, the techniques are random stuff they just kind of came up with and never examined. What if you're one of the few that actually thinks about 'How am I taking notes? Why and how did I study for this and what could have been better? Is there a better way for me to go through the semester so I'm prepared without having to do so much at the end? Is there something smarter I could be doing? How am I managing my schedule?'

It is like you treat school like a startup. Your product is grades and well-being, which you want to maximize, so you're constantly thinking about better ways to achieve it. Students who do that have a much better experience than those who say, 'I don't want to think about this.' Or those who just kind of do it and want to complain about how many hours they spend on studying and still got a bad grade."

Cal highlighted the fact that most people do not think to optimize. Just by adopting the habit of asking yourself how to optimize gives you a big head start in hacking any results you want. **My favorite way to optimize is to study people who have done what I want to achieve, identify the patterns, then apply those lessons.**

When Cal was in college, he was curious about how the top college students *became* top college students. There were students who had great grades, many meaningful experiences, and seemed to enjoy life at the same time. He then went on a journey to study and interview the superstar students in the country, hoping to find something other than talent that enabled these students to perform and enjoy life at a high level. He found great tips that helped him to graduate Dartmouth with an almost perfect GPA, to do meaningful projects while at school, and to publish two popular books sharing the information he gathered. If you are looking for more details on how to hack college, I highly recommend Newport's two books: *How to Win at College* and *How to be a Straight-A Student.* In addition, there are many other resources on accelerated learning and other topics relevant to college students. There are ample resources out there, but they're useless if you don't seek and use them.

How often do you ask yourself questions about your school work?

- What is the best way to do this?
- How can I optimize my schedule?
- How can I study more effectively?
- How can I make my health and energy as great as possible?
- How can I better cultivate great relationships?

You can see the pattern here. Do not forget this golden optimization question, **"How can I have the most badass college experience EVER?"**

## ACTION CHECKLIST

- ☐ Examine your goals for college and the approaches you are taking to reach those goals.
- ☐ How can you improve your approaches to optimize time and results?
- ☐ Find people who have created the results you want or resources they have created, and learn from them (seminars, books, videos, etc.).

# CHAPTER 9

# WHY DO YOU WANT TO BECOME AN ENTREPRENEUR?

———

*"Entrepreneurs are willing to work an 80-hour work week to avoid a 40-hour week."*

— LORI GREINER

*"Entrepreneurship is the hardest thing I have done in my whole life."*

— DAVID ROGIER

Every entrepreneur I interviewed asked me "Why do you want to be an entrepreneur?" If you want to be an entrepreneur just because it is cool, hot, and sexy, then it's time to rethink the reality of entrepreneurship.

Aaron Rasmussen, the Co-Founder of MasterClass (an online platform that offers people access to learn from the masters of different fields), said, "You need to know why you want to be an entrepreneur because the saying is true. Entrepreneurs are the people who are willing to work 80 hours a week to not work 40 hours a week. It is a tough path to pursue. And if your goal is to make more money or have more free time, statistics show that you are much better off being a senior executive at a big corporation than starting your own business."

An eye-opening reality is that Bloomberg estimates eight out of ten entrepreneurs who start businesses fail within the first 18 months.[1] **A whopping 80% crash and burn.** Another source indicates that 96% of businesses fail within ten years, and the ones that remain standing are not necessarily profitable.

Starting a company is hard. Heck, starting anything is hard. The journey of an entrepreneur is full of challenges, failures, hard work, and pressure from even your close friends and relatives. Without conviction and commitment, giving up seems like a logical option when hard times hit.

On the other hand, there are many successful founders who did not plan to become entrepreneurs. They simply committed to solving a problem they cared about, and entrepreneurship became a tool that served their purpose. Mark Zuckerberg emphasized that starting a company for the sake of starting a company is not a good way to go. Zuckerberg once said in an interview, "People decide often that they want to start a company before they decide what they want to do. And that feels really backwards to me."

**For me, entrepreneurship is attractive for many different reasons.** I love being judged by results versus the time I put in, solving problems creatively, challenging rules and status quo, and being in control of my life. I love turning ideas into reality. And most importantly, whenever I start something, I feel an enormous amount of energy, excitement, and happiness.

So why do *you* want to be an entrepreneur?

More money? More freedom? More power or control of your life? More free time? For love of building and starting things? To look cool? To be judged by your performance? To avoid having a boss? To avoid having a dress code? To control your own destiny? To face new challenges? To add value in a different way? The list can go on and on. **Don't stop until you find answers that are 100% congruent with who you are and what you want to do.**

As a bonus, here is an excerpt from inspirational list of quotations titled "The 12 Best Reasons to be an Entrepreneur," created by an expert in entrepreneurship, Roger Hamilton.[2]

1. The best way to predict the future is to create it. — Peter Drucker
2. Whatever the mind can conceive and believe, the mind can achieve. — Dr. Napoleon Hill
3. I think if you're an entrepreneur, you've got to dream big and then dream bigger. — Howard Schultz
4. If you can dream it, you can do it. — Walt Disney
5. Twenty years from now you will be more disappointed by the things that you didn't do than by the ones you did do. So throw off the bowlines. Sail away from the safe harbor. Catch the trade winds in your sails. Explore. Dream. Discover. — Mark Twain
6. You miss 100 percent of the shots you don't take. — Wayne Gretzky
7. Life shrinks or expands in proportion to one's courage. — Anais Nin
8. For a successful entrepreneur it can mean extreme wealth. But with extreme wealth comes extreme responsibility. And the responsibility for me is to invest in creating new businesses, create jobs, employ people, and to put money aside to tackle issues where we can make a difference. — Richard Branson
9. When you cease to dream you cease to live — Malcolm Forbes
10. Choose a job that you love, and you will never have to work a day in your life. — Confucius

## ACTION CHECKLIST

☐ Identify the top 3 reasons you want to become an entrepreneur.

☐ Write down all benefits that you believe entrepreneurship would bring. Examine them carefully to make sure you have an accurate understanding

## CHAPTER 10

# WHAT PROBLEMS DO YOU WANT TO SOLVE?

---

*"Going from PayPal, I thought: 'Well, what are some of the other problems that are likely to most affect the future of humanity?' Not from the perspective, 'What's the best way to make money?'"*

— ELON MUSK

*"If I had asked people what they wanted, they would have said faster horses."*

— HENRY FORD

The single biggest reason (36%) that startups fail is "building something nobody wants." In other words, building something that does not effectively solve important problems people have. The other three main reasons that startups fail are hiring poorly (18%), lack of focus (13%), and failing to market and sell (12%).[1]

Well, if we interpret lack of focus as lack of focus on solving the key problem, then **almost half of new businesses fail due to causes related to not able to solve customer's problems effectively.** Yet many entrepreneurs do not start by answering the key question: "What problem do I want to solve?" Being an entrepreneur starts there, and everything else comes after that.

Mark Zuckerberg told *Time Magazine*, "The most important thing that entrepreneurs should do is pick something they care about, work on it, but don't actually commit to turning it into a company until it actually works."[2]

Don't set out to build a company, he advised. Rather, "…start with the problem that you're trying to solve in the world…. The best companies that get built are things that are trying to drive some kind of social change, even if it's just local to one place."

Further, don't just identify a problem to solve — pick something you truly feel passionate about, he encouraged. "For anyone who's had the experience of actually building a company, you know that you go through some really hard things along the way, and I think part of what gets you through that is believing in what you're doing and knowing that what you're doing is really delivering a lot of value for people," Zuckerberg explained. "And that's how the best companies end up getting made."[3]

Stop thinking about what company you want to start. Instead, find a problem you care about solving and start to make things better.

I learned a helpful technique from Katie Meyler during an interview. Katie is the founder of the charity organization "More Than Me," and she was awarded 2014 TIME Person of the Year for her contributions on the front lines of solving the Ebola epidemic. "Lock yourself in a room for a day. Imagine if you had a gun to your head, and if you do not come up with a problem you are passionate about solving and the first three steps you are going to take to solve this problem, you will die. I sometimes add pressure and think my loved ones will also suffer if I do not come up with an answer in the time frame."

A fun fact is Katie is also one of the "accidental entrepreneurs." She did not have a background in business and hadn't even thought about being a founder. This changed when a girl asked for Katie's help to go to school during Katie's volunteering work in Liberia. This girl who was doing sex work in exchange for clean drinking water at eleven years old. Katie helped as much as she could. Then, more and more, little girls came to Katie for help. Since Katie didn't find anyone else who cared about this issue enough to take action, she ended up spending more time and energy on solving this problem that touched her heart. Today, More Than Me runs about 200 public schools in Liberia and impacts more than 50,000 children.

Need more inspiration? Uber started when the founders couldn't hail a taxi on a snowy night in Paris. Airbnb started when the founders were looking to get some cash by renting out the air-mattress in their living room. Microsoft was founded to solve the problem of complex computer interface, which was the main barrier stopping people from owning personal computers.

So, what problem do you want to solve?

## ACTION CHECKLIST

☐ Use the "If you had a gun to your head" exercise. Identify 3 small problems and 3 big problems you want to solve.

☐ Start to look at the world with curiosity and entrepreneurial eyes. Identify at least 1 problem you want to solve each month.

☐ Keep a journal about these ideas and continue to develop solutions to the problems you care most about.

☐ Start actually DOING something about these problems.

## PART 2

# WHAT TO LEARN

CHAPTER 11

# LEADING YOUR OWN SHIP

———

*"Leadership is leading your own ship."*

— ANAND CHULANI

*"It is in your moments of decision that your destiny is shaped."*

— TONY ROBBINS

Have you ever wondered "Why we do what we do?" This question really made me curious. Initially, it was because you can't really hack a system without understanding it first. Hence, it is hard to change a behavior in the long run if we don't understand why we behave the old way in the first place. On the other hand, it is a tremendous advantage if we know how to influence our emotions and behaviors by understanding what influences us. **Once you know how to lead your own ship (yourself), then you can lead a fleet to make anything happen.**

In this chapter, I distilled the key concepts from Tony Robbins' work on this subject. Tony is a great person to learn from on this topic because his curiosity about why people do what they do has led him to spend decades seeking the answer. In the past four decades, he has worked with millions of people around the world and gained powerful insights about human psychology.

## DECISIONS SHAPE DESTINY

This might sound heavy, but think about it. What were the two or three important decisions you made in the last decade of your life that shaped where you are today? If you made those decisions differently, how would your life be different? They could be big decisions such as where to study, where to work, and who to be in a relationship with. Or they could be small decisions, such as start to work out that led to a big change in your physical well-being. Furthermore, we make hundreds of decisions each day that adds up to affect the course of our lives.

In order to understand the decisions we make, we have to examine what shapes decisions? The answer consists of two parts, your emotional state in the short run, and your model of the world in the long run.

## YOUR EMOTIONAL STATE

The emotional state is the sum of the emotions that you experience, and it's a factor that's been overlooked by most people. Tony gave a fun example to demonstrate why emotional states are so powerful.

Have you ever had this experience? You did something, and after, you thought to yourself, "I can't believe I said or did that; that was so stupid." We have all done that right? On the other hand. Have you done something, and after it, you proudly went, "That was me!" It wasn't your ability; it was your state. To put it simply, would your action be different if you were angry, or happy, or excited, or anxious, or sad? Of course. This is why state is the most powerful factor that influences us in the short run.

## OWNING YOUR EMOTIONAL STATE

What creates the emotional states we experience? Wouldn't it be cool to be able to tap into any emotions at any time and anywhere once we know the answer?

According to Tony, the three things that influence our state is the 'Triad." To change or create a state, you need to change your focus, physiology, or language. If you change all of these, you are guaranteed to be in a different state.

One part of the Triad is your **focus**. Whatever we focus on, we feel. If you focus on people you love or people you dislike right now, you will have two very different emotions. Two people can go through the same event and have totally different experiences because they focus on different things. For example, two people experience a car accident in the same car. One can focus on everyone in the car is unharmed and feel grateful, while another may focus on how they were frightened, blame the other driver, and feel angry. Your life is controlled by your focus. That's why you need to focus on where you want to go, not on what you fear.

The second part of the triad is your **physiology**. Whatever you're feeling right now is directly related to how you're using your body. **Emotion is created by motion**. If you slump your shoulders, lean your head forward, and look down, you'll move toward a state of sadness. However, the next time you find yourself in a negative state, if you stand up, throw your shoulders back, and take a few deep breaths, you will find that you're able to put yourself in a more resourceful state. Do you feel stressed? Workout for five minutes and you will feel stronger mentally. Changing your body is the quickest way to change your emotions.

The third part of the triad is **language**. Language covers a broad range, but the main thing to focus on is the questions you ask yourself, either aloud or inside your head. If you ask, "Why does this always have to happen to me?"—you will create a much different set of emotions than if you asked, "How can I benefit from this?" or "Where's the gift in this?" or "What's humorous about this?" The language patterns you run play a significant role in the meaning you give a situation—and the emotion that situation creates in you

## MODEL OF THE WORLD

Your model of the world is what shapes you long term. Your model of the world is the filter and what shapes you. Your worldview is what causes you to make the decisions you do. To change, you need to understand what influences you. There are two aspects of your model of the world that you need to consider: how you fulfill your needs and what you believe.

### *FIRST, WHAT'S YOUR TARGET?*
### *WHAT ARE YOU AFTER?*

It's not your desires. You can get your desires or goals and wonder is this all there is? What influences you are the way you meet the human needs that drive all of our actions. There are the six universal human needs that Tony has identified:

1.  **Certainty** — the need for safety, stability, security, comfort, order, predictability, control, and consistency.

2.  **Uncertainty or Variety** — the need for variety, surprise, challenges, excitement, difference, chaos, adventure, change, and novelty.

3.  **Significance** — the need to have meaning, to be special, needed, wanted, and worthy as well as a sense of pride or importance .

4.  **Love and Connection** — the need for communication, unity, approval and attachment — to feel connected with, intimate, and loved by other human beings.

5.  **Growth** — the need for emotional, intellectual, and spiritual development.

6.  **Contribution** — the need to give beyond ourselves, to give, care, protect and serve others.

The main differences between people are due to the different needs they value the most. Imagine a person who values certainty as their No. 1 need, in contrast to someone who values uncertainty the most. How different would they be? Very different, right? One wants to be safe and loves routine, while the other craves adventure and loves surprises. How would they make decisions? Their choices would be very different, for sure. Tony believes your top two needs significantly influence who you are and what you do. People not only have different needs, but also different ways they go about fulfilling those needs. For example, you can fulfill your need for significance by being the best in something, making a difference, talking down on others, or pretending to be better than others. The first two choices are positive, while the last two are negative.

## SECOND, AFTER YOU KNOW WHAT YOU WANT, HOW DO YOU GET THERE?

This is where beliefs come in. Your beliefs are like a GPS system that guides you to your goal. There are two kinds of beliefs.

Global beliefs are your beliefs about big things, your generalizations. To discover your global beliefs, finish these sentences:

- Life is...
- People are...
- Work is...
- Rich people are...

Got it? Any generalizations you make are your global beliefs about the world. Consider how people who believe that "life is a party" will very different from people who believe that "life is a test. Or people who believe "people are nice" versus "people are greedy"?

The second type of beliefs are situational, and they are made up of if-then statements in your brain. For example, if I want to be fit, then I must eat clean 100% of the time, workout every day, and have superhuman discipline. This kind of limiting belief makes it very hard for a person to take action because it is almost impossible to achieve. More limiting beliefs might be that I am not disciplined enough to be fit, health is decided by genetics, or I do not have time to take care of myself. I probably won't achieve my goal due to these limiting beliefs. It is like your beliefs guarantee you can never get to where you want to go. How fun is that? On the other hand, there are empowering beliefs that make us stronger. We all have both. It's best to work toward beliefs that empower you. There is so much that can be covered on this topic, including how to change your beliefs. Read *Awaken the Giant Within* to learn more.

The first step of changing or creating anything is to be aware of it. It gives you a tremendous advantage because you are aware some powerful invisible influences that most people didn't know existed. The second step is to start applying these hacks and lead yourself to your best state and performance when any situation requires it. Welcome aboard a very different ship.

## ACTION CHECKLIST

- ☐ Consider all the "states" that you have. Choose 2 of your most empowering and disempowering states.
- ☐ Use the Triad to recognize what you do, say, or focus on to reach these states.

☐ Practice using that "personal recipe" to create the best state that you can.

☐ Consider which of the 6 Needs that you favor most. Think about whether these are the needs that you want to be your "Top 2."

☐ Examine your belief system. What are your Global Beliefs?

☐ Make a list of the most empowering and limiting beliefs you have? What beliefs do you want to add? What beliefs can you eliminate?

☐ Research and read more about this topic to create the life you want to lead!

CHAPTER 12

# RESOURCEFULNESS

———

*"The defining factor is never resources; it's resourcefulness."*

— TONY ROBBINS

*Life's too short to hang out with people who aren't resourceful.*

— JEFF BEZOS

"If you ask people, 'Why didn't you achieve...something?'
What do they tell you?" The TED Talk speaker asked this
question to an audience full of accomplished individuals.
Answers from the audience included, "Not enough money"
and "Not enough time." There were several answers along
the lines of "Didn't have X (something)." Then someone
shouted, "I didn't have enough Supreme Court Judges." The
entire room, including the speaker, broke into laughter, as
the camera turned on former Vice President Al Gore. The

speaker, Tony Robbins, gave Al Gore a high five.

The speaker continued, "What do all the answers you gave have in common?" Resources. People usually blame missing a goal on lack of one resource or another. The defining factor is never resources; it's resourcefulness. Specifically, if people tap into their emotions, they find a level of passion that will crush any goal.

## EMOTION IS THE ULTIMATE RESOURCE

If we tap into the right emotion, we can get ourselves to do anything. If you're creative, playful, and fun enough, you can be attractive to just about anyone. If you are determined, creative, and flexible enough, you will find the way to get what you want, and you will find a solution to any problem.

You may have wondered why people with amazing resources failed. Why do people who were born into well-off families, who went to great colleges, or who work at good companies often don't succeed? On the other hand, there are people who come from harsh backgrounds with almost no resources, and they end up achieving incredible things. The reason is as Tony Robbins said in this TED talk, "The defining factor is never resources; it's resourcefulness."

Being resourceful is about tapping into the right emotions

and mindset to find the resources you need. The following stories illustrate this.

## CEREAL SAVED AIRBNB FROM BANKRUPTCY

In the midst of a presidential election campaign, Brian and his co-founders, Joe and Nathan, were working on their startup—renting out air beds and breakfast—but their company, Airbnb, was struggling. They had maxed out a wallet full of credit cards and were tens of thousands of dollars in debt.

That's when they came up with the idea of selling cereal instead: "In debt and desperate one midnight, we had the idea if the 'air beds' in 'air bed and breakfast' wasn't working, maybe we can sell 'breakfast' instead." Unfortunately, all the big cereal producers laughed at their idea of making president-themed cereal (Obama O's and Cap'n McCain's). Undaunted, Brian, Joe, and Nathan went to the local grocery store, bought cereal, and repackaged it in custom boxes. They folded and glued 1000 boxes by hand. They numbered each box as a "limited edition" and sold each box at $40 a box. Brian says, "We sold $30,000 worth of cereal and this is how we funded the company and came up with the phrase 'be a cereal entrepreneur.'"

Without that money, the company may not have survived. But it was more than the cash that came from the idea. Brian and Joe interviewed with the famous Silicon Valley startup accelerator, Y Combinator, but the interview wasn't going well. So Joe pulled out a box of Obama O's and offered some to Paul Graham, Y Combinator founder. "What's this?" Paul asked. When they explained, Paul's reaction was priceless: "Wait, you guys funded your company based on selling breakfast cereal?" Paul sensed there was a market crash coming (which hit just a few months later) and said he was looking for founders who would survive the crash. "Wow. You guys are like cockroaches. You just won't die." Paul said, "If you can convince people to pay $40 for a box of cereal, you can probably convince them to pay to sleep on each other's air mattresses. You guys are in."

## HOW MUCH COULD YOU MAKE WITH $5 AND TWO HOURS?

How much could you make with $5 and two hours? Tina Seelig is the executive director of the Stanford Technology Ventures Program, where she gave her students this exact question. The result was an average 4,000% return! The rules specify that each team gets $5, the team can plan for as long as they want, but once the teams start spending money, they only have two hours to measure the return. A few days later, each team presents their results to the class.

Here's a clue: the teams that made the most money didn't use the five dollars at all. They realized that focusing on the money actually framed the problem way too tightly. They decided to reinterpret the problem more broadly. They changed the question to: "What can we do to make money if we start with absolutely nothing?"

One group identified the problem of frustratingly long lines at popular restaurants on Saturday night. The team decided to help those people who didn't want to wait in line by selling people the spots in the line. Another team set up a stand that offered to measure bicycle tire pressure for free. If the tires needed filling, they added air for one dollar. After some observation, the team stopped asking for a specific payment and requested donations instead. Their income soared.

The team that generated the greatest profit looked at the resources at their disposal through a completely different lens and made $650. These students determined that the most valuable asset they had was neither the $5 nor the two hours. Instead, their most precious resource was their three-minute presentation time on Monday. They decided to sell it to a company that wanted to recruit the students in the class. The team created a three-minute "commercial" for that company and showed it to the students during the time of their presentation. They recognized that they had a fabulously valuable asset—that others didn't even notice—just waiting to be mined." What a cool story!

## THERE ARE DIFFERENT KINDS OF RESOURCES

How do great entrepreneurs always manage to give more than they take and still end up with more? By knowing the difference between scarcity and value. When you share a scarce resource, you end up with less. Share your money, and you end up with less money. Share your time, and you end up with less time. **When you share an entrepreneurial resource (value), you end up with more.** Share your best ideas, and the idea will grow as others add to it. Share your connections, and your connections grow in strength and size. In turn, your entrepreneurial resources can be traded for scarce resources and, in time, you'll have all the time and money you need.[1]

Your vision, mission, trust, reputation, passion, power, determination, responsibility, experience, wisdom, happiness, care, and love are all valuable entrepreneurial resources that grow exponentially the more you share them. Focus on scarce resources, and you will never have enough. Focus on your entrepreneurial resources and you will always have more than enough.

## ACTION CHECKLIST

☐ Make a list of what you can deliver of value, with no "start-up" money.

☐ Practice being resourceful by always thinking of at least 3 ways to solve a problem or approach a subject.

☐ Inventory all your skills and values as resources. Remember to appreciate your creativity.

## CHAPTER 13

# THE SUBTLE ART OF NOT GIVING A F*CK

———

*"You only get a limited number of fucks to give over your lifetime, so you must spend them with care."*

— MARK MANSON

Do you obsess about what other people think of you? Do you get angry at the driver that cut you off? Does fear of failure stop you from trying? It seems like you're giving too many fucks. (We all do it. I'm super guilty of doing this myself.)

As time passes, I start to taste the sense of happiness and freedom that comes from not giving a fuck. When I get myself to care less about how other people think about me, the confidence and calmness I feel are **unshakable**. On the other hand, when I care too much about project or interview that really won't matter a year from now, I feel stressed and life seems to be sucked out of me. The ability to give fewer fucks is especially important for entrepreneurs because this is a bumpy road less traveled by. Most people would not support your decision to be an entrepreneur. Most people won't think your idea is going to work. There will be many failures and disappointment waiting to happen. If we care about them too much, there will be no energy to do the real work and persist.

In short, I want to get better at not giving a fuck about unimportant things, and that's what Mark Manson's book *The Subtle Art of Not Giving a Fuck* is all about. Here are some excerpts of wisdom from the book in Mark's voice.

## THE PROBLEM

The point is, most of us struggle throughout our lives by giving too many fucks in situations where fucks do not deserve to be given. We give a fuck about the rude gas station attendant, TV shows, and why our friends don't bother asking us about our awesome weekend. We give a fuck when it's raining, and we were supposed to go jogging in the morning.[1]

Fucks given everywhere. And for what purpose? For what reason? Convenience? Easy comforts? A pat on the fucking back maybe? This is the problem, my friend.

## LEARNING THE ART OF NOT GIVING A F*CK [2]

The ability to reserve our fucks for only the most fuckworthy of situations would surely make life a hell of a lot easier. Failure would be less terrifying. Rejection less painful. I mean, if we could only give a few less fucks, or a few more consciously-directed fucks, then life would feel pretty fucking easy. **What we don't realize is that there is a fine art of non-fuck-giving.**

People aren't just born not giving a fuck. In fact, we're born giving way too many fucks. Ever watch a kid cry his eyes out because his hat is the wrong shade of blue? Developing the ability to control and manage the fucks you give is the essence of strength and integrity. We must craft and hone our lack of fuckery over the course of years and decades.

### SUBTLETY #1: NOT GIVING A FUCK DOES NOT MEAN BEING INDIFFERENT; IT MEANS BEING COMFORTABLE WITH BEING DIFFERENT

When most people envision giving no fucks, they envision a kind of perfect and serene indifference to everything. People who are indifferent are lame and scared. My mother was recently screwed out of a large chunk of money by a close friend. Had I been indifferent, I would have shrugged my shoulders and moved on. But instead, I was pissed off. I said, "No, screw that, Mom, we're going to a lawyer and go after this asshole. Why? Because I don't give a fuck. I will ruin this guy's life if I have to."

When we say, "Damn, watch out, Mark Manson just don't give a fuck," we don't mean that Mark Manson doesn't care about anything; on the contrary. What we mean is that Mark Manson doesn't care about adversity in the face of his goals, he doesn't care about pissing some people off to do what he feels is right or important or noble.

## SUBTLETY #2: TO NOT GIVE A FUCK ABOUT ADVERSITY, YOU MUST FIRST GIVE A FUCK ABOUT SOMETHING MORE IMPORTANT THAN ADVERSITY

Eric Hoffer once wrote: "A man is likely to mind his own business when it is worth minding. When it is not, he takes his mind off his own meaningless affairs by minding other people's business." If you find yourself consistently giving too many fucks about trivial shit that bothers you—your ex-girlfriend's new Facebook picture, how quickly the batteries die in the TV remote, missing out the sale on hand sanitizer—chances are you don't have much going on in your life to give a legitimate fuck about. And that's your real problem. Not the hand sanitizer.

## SUBTLETY #3: WE ALL HAVE A LIMITED NUMBER OF FUCKS TO GIVE; PAY ATTENTION TO WHO YOU GIVE THEM

Maturity is what happens when one learns to only give a fuck about what's truly fuckworthy. It's nice; you should try it sometime. People who don't give a fuck say, "fuck it," not to everything in life, but rather they say "Fuck it" to everything unimportant in life. They reserve their fucks for what truly fucking matters. Friends. Family. Purpose. Burritos. And an occasional lawsuit or two. And because of that, because they reserve their fucks for only the big things, the important things, people give a fuck about them in return.

## YOU ARE *NOT* SPECIAL

After decades of cultural conditioning of everyone is the best, our generation became entitled. Entitled people only see their positives. They can't acknowledge their problems and weaknesses. There's nothing wrong with trying to become exceptional at something. However, you need to realize first that you're only mediocre. Stop taking yourself too seriously. You are not under a spotlight. Stop giving a fuck about failing, making mistake, embarrassing yourself, asking for help, getting rejected. You are not special. It's O.K.to be mediocre. If you tried and failed to become exceptional, who gives a fuck?

## ACTION CHECKLIST

- ☐ Start to observe yourself and notice what do you give a fuck about.
- ☐ Make a list of the 5 important things you actually should give a fuck about.
- ☐ Stop giving a fuck about unimportant things, including adversity.

# CHAPTER 14

# ENJOY LIFE

———

*"Life is too short to suffer."*

— TONY ROBBINS

*"The Constitution only gives people the right to pursue happiness. You have to catch it yourself."*

— BENJAMIN FRANKLIN

Tim Ferris asked some of his closest friends, some of whom are the most accomplished people in the world, "What should I do with my life?"

The answer? "Enjoy it." This simple yet profound message touched my heart. Please pause and let that sink in.

"What if enjoying life became the biggest accomplishment

in life?" My brain didn't quite get it when I first heard this question from Tony Robbins. Then I thought, well if that's the case, I am doing a pretty bad job at life. Judging by the fact that you picked up this book and have read this far, you are probably an over-achiever too.

The upside is that our drive and hunger push us to get better and improve, but the downside is we spend a lot of time being stressed and dissatisfied. But seriously, stop to think about this for a minute; **what is the point of achieving things if the experience is not enjoyable?**

The most powerful tool and framework on how to enjoy life I've found are from Tony Robbins; he teaches that we need to learn to live in a beautiful state. The following information is based on Tony's newest book, *Unshakable: Your Financial Freedom Playbook.*

## THE MOST IMPORTANT DECISION OF YOUR LIFE[1]

Tony Robbins says his thinking has evolved, that he now believes that there is only one important question in life. **Are you committed to being happy, no matter what happens to you?**

To put this another way, will you commit to enjoying life not only when everything goes your way but also when everything goes against you, when injustice happens, when someone screws you over, when you lose something or someone you love, or when nobody seems to understand or appreciate you? **Unless we make this definitive decision to stop suffering and live in a beautiful state, our survival minds will create suffering whenever our desires, expectations, or preferences are not met.** What a waste of so much of our lives!

**This is a decision that can change everything in your life, starting today.** But it's not enough just to say that you'd like to make this change or that your preference is to be happy no matter what. You have to own this decision, do whatever it takes to make it happen, and cut off any possibility of turning back. It comes down to drawing a line in the sand today and declaring, **"I'm done with suffering. I'm going to live every day to the fullest and find juice in every moment, including the ones I don't like, because life is just too short to suffer."**

## BEAUTIFUL STATE VERSUS SUFFERING[2]

In Tony's words, "the mental and emotional state in which you live is ultimately the result of where you choose to focus your thoughts." We can choose to live in one of two states of mind: a beautiful state or a suffering state.

The human brain isn't designed to make us happy and fulfilled. It's designed to make us survive.

This two-million-year-old organ is always looking for what's wrong, for whatever can hurt us, so that we can either fight it or take flight from it. If you and I leave this ancient survival software to run the show, what chance do we have of enjoying life? **An undirected mind operates naturally in survival mode, constantly identifying and magnifying potential threats to our well-being.** The result is a life filled with stress and anxiety.

Most people live this way since it's the path of least resistance. They make unconscious decisions, based on habit and conditioning, and are at the mercy of their own minds. They assume that it's just an inevitable part of life to get frustrated, stressed, sad, and angry—in other words, to live in a suffering state. But I'm happy to tell you there's another path: one that involves directing your thoughts so that your mind does your bidding, not the other way around.

Now, before we go any further, let's just clarify the difference between these two emotional and mental states:

## A BEAUTIFUL STATE

When you feel love, joy, gratitude, awe, playfulness, creativity, or appreciation, that is when you're in a beautiful state. In this state, you know exactly what to do, and you do the right thing. In this state, your spirit and your heart are alive, and the best of you comes out. Nothing feels like a problem and everything flows. You feel no fear or frustration. You're in harmony with your true essence.

## A SUFFERING STATE

When you're feeling stressed out, worried, frustrated, angry, depressed, overwhelmed, or fearful, you're in a suffering state. We've all experienced these and countless other "negative" emotions, even if we're not always keen to admit it! Most achievers much prefer to think they're stressed rather than fearful. However, **"stress" is just the achiever's word for fear.** If I follow the trail of your stress, it'll take me to your deepest fear.

Everyone has his or her own flavor of suffering. So here's my question for you: what's your favorite flavor of suffering? Which energy-sapping emotion do you indulge in most? Is it sadness? Frustration? Anger? Worry? The specific details don't really matter because they're all states of suffering. And all this suffering is really just the result of an undirected mind that's hell-bent on looking for problems.

Consciously or unconsciously, you're focused on at least one of three triggers for suffering:

## 1. SUFFERING TRIGGER IS "LOSS"

When you focus on loss, you become convinced that a particular problem has caused or will cause you to lose something you value.

## 2. SUFFERING TRIGGER IS "LESS"

When you focus on the idea that you have less or will have less, you will suffer.

## 3. SUFFERING TRIGGER IS "NEVER"

When you focus on the idea or become consumed by a belief that you'll never have something you value—such as love, joy, respect, wealth, opportunity—you're doomed to suffer, you'll never be happy, you'll never become the person you want to be. This pattern of perception is a surefire route to pain.

These three patterns of focus account for most, if not all, of our suffering. And you know what's crazy? It doesn't even matter if the problem is real or not! Whatever we focus on, we feel—regardless of what actually happened.

But here's the good news: once you're aware of these patterns of focus, you can systematically change them, thereby freeing yourself from these habits of suffering. It all starts with the realization that this involves a conscious choice. Either you master your mind or it masters you.

## HOW TO LIVE IN A BEAUTIFUL STATE NOW?

### *"TRADE YOUR EXPECTATION FOR APPRECIATION"*

Tony says the fastest way to change your life is to trade your expectation for appreciation. Gratitude is the ultimate antidote to stress. You simply can't be grateful and suffer at the same time. The honest truth is, if you are reading this book right now, your life has already been blessed in so many ways. Whenever I feel stressed or in a bad state, if I start to focus on what I can be grateful for, the suffering just goes away. It works wonders.

### *FOCUS ON OTHERS*

You can stop the pattern of being triggered by fear by focusing on others. How are they doing? How can you help? What can you do to make someone's day? Serving others helps you to remember your own value, and realize how much you have to share.

### ACTION CHECKLIST

☐ Start to notice and identify moments of suffering. Become aware of your "favorite" patterns of suffering.

☐ Begin a gratitude journal to start living in a beautiful state.

☐ Imagine the life you will live in a beautiful state; not about what you'll have, but how you'll feel, no matter what. Write about the perfect day.

CHAPTER 15

# MEDITATE WITHOUT FALLING ASLEEP

———

*"You should sit in meditation for 20 minutes a day, unless you are too busy. Then you should sit for an hour."*

— OLD ZEN SAYING

*"We do not rise to the level of our expectations. We fall to the level of our training."*

— ARCHILOCHUS

In his latest book *Tool of Titans*, Tim Ferriss identified what he calls the "Most Consistent Pattern of All." "**More than 80% of the world-class performers I've interviewed have some form of daily meditation or mindfulness practice.** Both can be thought of as "cultivating a present-state awareness that helps you to be nonreactive." This applies to everyone from Arnold Schwarzenegger to Justin Boreta of *The Glitch Mob*, and from elite athletes like Amelia Boone to writers like Maria Popova.[1]

Tim calls it a "meta-skill" that improves everything else."

Most of us have heard of the benefits of meditation around stress-reduction. Maybe the benefits associated with productivity and creativity are sometimes overlooked.

Billionaire Ray Dalio, the founder hedge-fund behemoth Bridgewater Associates, is considered the most successful hedge fund manager of all time. He's also been practicing Transcendental Meditation for more than 40 years. "When I look back at my life, I am happy to have had what most people would consider a successful life, not only in terms of business, but in my relationships and in lots of ways. More than anything else, I attribute it to meditation—partially because of the creativity, partly because of the centeredness. TM has given me an ability to put things in perspective, which has helped a lot. I think meditation has been the single biggest influence on my life." Dalio mentioned in another interview that meditation calms the part of our brain called amygdala, which controls our response to fear or stress (fight or flight). And in a high-stress and sometimes chaotic world of entrepreneurship, the ability to stay calm and centered is extra valuable.[2]

One of my influential mentors, Ari, an entrepreneur and founder of a private equity firm with a focus on real estate, got passionately serious about meditation during our conversation over email.

"Antonia, have you learned how to meditate?"

"Well, I have meditated before, but I haven't had formal training."

"Go learn meditation, preferably Transcendental Meditation. It will change your life! It changed mine. The benefits and results will blow your mind!"

I was physically in China when I got his email. But when a mentor like Ari says something is "life-changing," I pay attention and take action. I looked up the closest TM center to my summer internship place in NYC so that I could make learning TM the first thing I did when I got back to the States.

I took the courses for four nights, and many of my classmates noticed changes in just two days. Since that summer of 2016, I have started meditating twice a day, and I noticed obvious changes after the meditation sessions, especially after the afternoon sessions. Some afternoons, I feel a stuck sensation, feeling overwhelmed and irritated from the amount of information or stress that have accumulated over the workday, and this pressure keeps me from concentrating and creating meaningful work. I also feel some annoying physical sensa-tions as well. **After my 20-minute meditation session, I normally feel physically and mentally relaxed and refreshed. I feel the stress melt away and my perception opening up again.** When I open my eyes after the session, the world seems to have brighter colors, and I am looking at the world from a different perspective. While I have not been perfect with my meditation routine, using the excuses of I'm too busy, I have discovered that scheduling the meditation time into my calendar and reminding myself of the benefits have helped me stay on track.

There are many options you can choose to meditate (some recommend by Tim Ferriss):

- Use an app like Headspace or Calm.
- Listen to a guided meditation from Sam Harris, Tara Brach, or others available online.
- Take a TM course (tm.org). (The cost is the main drawback for TM. It will cost around $1000 in the US (half price for students), but this option offers a coach and accountability. TM is a non-profit organization offers financial support to some cases.)
- If you want to try mantra-based meditation without a course, you can sit and silently repeat one two-syllable word ("na-ture" or "o-m") for 10 to 20 minutes first thing in the morning.
- Just simply sit still and focus on observing your breath. Notice your thoughts and let them go without getting engaged in them.

## ENCOURAGEMENT FROM TIM FERRIS

"If you spend even a second noticing this wandering and bringing your attention back to your mantra (or whatever), that is a "successful" session. As Tara Brach pointed out to me, the muscle you're working is bringing your attention back to something. My sessions are 99% monkey mind, but it's the other 1% that matters. **If you're getting frustrated, your standards are too high or your sessions are too long.** Once again, for seven days, rig the game so you can win. The goal is not to "quiet the mind," which will give your brain a hyperactive tantrum; the goal is to observe your thoughts. If you're replaying some bullshit in your head and notice it, just say, "Thinking, thinking" to yourself and return to your focus. Done consistently, my reward for meditating is getting 30% to 50% more done in a day with 50% less stress. Why? Because I have already done a warmup in recovering from distraction: my morning sit. If I later get distracted or interrupted during work hours, I can return to my primary task far more quickly and completely."[3]

## ACTION CHECKLIST

- ☐ Pick a meditation method or program.
- ☐ Meditate at least for 10 minutes every day (preferably in the morning).
- ☐ Meditate for at least seven straight days and judge the results for yourself.

CHAPTER 16

# WIN THE WAR OVER PROCRASTINATION

---

*"Most of us have two lives. The life we live, and the unlived life within us. The two stand in Resistance."*

— STEVEN PRESSFIELD

*"You may delay, but time will not."*

— BENJAMIN FRANKLIN

Have you ever had a dream that you wanted to pursue—but didn't? Have you ever had a great idea with lots of potential—but failed to take action? Have you ever started a new gym routine, diet, project or program of any kind—but failed to follow through on it?

If you answered "yes" to any of the questions, then you're in the same boat as everyone else—suffering from what Pressfield refers to as "Resistance." Steven Pressfield is the author of best-selling book *The War of Art: Breakthrough the Blocks and Win Your Inner Creative Battles*, a book focused on overcoming resistance.

We've all been there. Resistance occurs when we try to break away from something old (a bad habit, a crappy career) in search of something new and better. Anything that requires any amount of willpower, discipline, or fear-facing is a threat to Resistance, and Resistance doesn't like that very much. Resistance is hesitation. Resistance is procrastination. Resistance is the voice that says, "You can't." Resistance is the very thing that prevents us from doing what we're meant to do more than anything else.[1]

Resistance is something that I have been battling with for a long time. I hate the feeling of being stuck, trying to avoid work, yet knowing work has to be done. It's an awful feeling, of being powerless. Then I let this feeling become an excuse to keep distracting myself from doing real work. After that, I would feel even worse about myself, and more stressed about doing the work because I just wasted precious time. It is a vicious cycle.

The Resistance I experienced on a daily basis was magnified during this book writing experience: my first big attempt to create some meaningful content. I kept telling myself, "I will have the weekend to get so much writing done," and kept finding myself only writing about 500 words during the whole weekend.

So what did I do during the weekend? Well, I didn't really have fun since I was busy trying to avoid writing and justifying my actions. The result? I felt more stressed, stuck, and powerless. This, by the way, is not a great way to start writing productively. As the process went on, I began to realize that the first 30 mins of writing was the hardest. I battled with all the distracting temptations, a million different things, and I gave in most of the time. But during the rare instances of me making it through, I started to be able to focus and let my thoughts flow.

Even the best and most experienced among us feel Resistance on a regular basis. For example, Pressfield writes about how actor/entertainer Henry Fonda would throw up prior to every performance. Fonda has been on stage several hundred times...did Resistance stop him? No. He battled with Resistance prior to every single show. And he won every battle with Resistance by accepting the fact that it was a natural occurrence for anyone doing anything they care deeply for.

To help you beat your Resistance, I'm including three hacks to overcome resistance and procrastination.

## PRESSFIELD'S GUIDELINES

1. Define your dreams (whatever you want to do most in life).
2. Stay committed to your craft.
3. Beat Resistance with perspiration, not inspiration. Resistance fears commitment, craft, and dedication.
4. Be a professional: show up on time, put in the hours, be in it for the long game.
5. "I write only when inspiration strikes. Fortunately, it strikes every morning at nine o'clock sharp." — W. Somerset Maugham
6. Accept the fact that Resistance is something you're going to have to live with, and that the best way to prevent it from paralyzing you, is to face it, feel it, and take action in spite of it.[2]

## BEATING PROCRASTINATION WHEN STUDYING

1. Never say "I am going to study." Always plan out what exactly you will be doing (like reading for English class for an hour, or doing Economics homework for an hour); be specific about what, when, where, and for how long.
2. Study for 30 mins as a chunk in a distraction-free zone. No texting, social media, browsing, in that 30 mins. Take a 5-10 min break in between.
3. Chunk it better. Chunking basically means group similar activities together. Change and simplify the way you think of one activity you are trying to do. Complexity is the enemy of execution.

4. Schedule enough time for important activities early in the day. This way you won't get "too busy" to do something

## THE FIVE-SECOND RULE

Mel Robbins discovered this hack as a tool that turned her life around. With her popular book *The 5 Second Rule: Transform Your Life, Work, and Confidence with Everyday Courage* and TED talks, Robbins is helping millions of people to overcome resistance. Though it seems like an overly simple or even trivial idea, I highly recommend this powerful practice.

Focus on the idea you have to do something good (work, exercise, speak up, meet with your boss, get out of bed, etc.)

1. Focus on the idea you have to do something good (work, exercise, speak up, meet with your boss, get out of bed, and etc.)
2. Countdown 5, 4, 3, 2, 1…
3. Then take immediate, physical action toward what you want to do. (Or your brain will most likely talk you out of doing whatever you intend to do.)

## ACTION CHECKLIST

☐ Do something you've been procrastinating on NOW.
☐ Start to use the Five-Second Rule to get yourself to take 1 immediate action a week.

☐ Make a list of things that you've procrastinated completing—and experiment with these methods to find out what works best for you.

☐ CELEBRATE! Enjoy winning at overcoming resistance!

CHAPTER 17

# TIME MANAGEMENT

———

*"My favorite things in life don't cost any money. It's really clear that the most precious resource we all have is time."*

— STEVE JOBS

*"Wasted time is more expensive than wasted money."*

— PAULO COELHO

Imagine that you are given $86,400 every day. At the end of the day, all the money you have left goes to zero. There is only one rule: you cannot save money. What would you do? Well, the only viable option would be to spend it, and hopefully you spend it well.

Of course, you are not given $86,400 every day, but you are given 86,400 seconds. If you have the time to spend, the only question is how well do you spend it? The way you spend your time is the way you spend your life. LinkedIn Founder Reid Hoffman suggests that review your calendar, journals, and old emails to get a sense for how you spent your last six Saturdays. What do you do when you have nothing urgent to do? How you spend your free time may reveal your true interests and aspirations; compare them to what you say your aspirations are. If your schedule doesn't reflect on your values and priorities, it's a good time to adjust and refocus.

In *On the Shortness of Life*, the philosopher Seneca wrote, "People are frugal in guarding their personal property; but as soon as it comes to squandering time, they are most wasteful of the one thing in which it is right to be stingy." Based on my observations, most people, including myself, do not treat time with proper respect. Seneca continued, "You live as if you were destined to live forever, no thought of your frailty ever enters your head, of how much time has already gone by you take no heed. You squander time as if you drew from a full and abundant supply, though all the while that day which you bestow on some person or thing is perhaps your last."[1]

The first and most important step to time management? Start to treat time as your most precious resource, which it is.

When I interviewed Seth Goldman, the co-founder of Honest Tea, he also emphasized time management as an important skill for students to learn. Being an entrepreneur will require people to handle many things at the same time, and college is a great practice ground for that. When Seth was in college, he was on the track team, a political organization, and running his own projects. He took on a lot of things, and he believes it was beneficial because he learned how to juggle and manage multiple things at one time.

We are not going to cover more traditional time management tips here to help you fill every minute of your day and cross off more "to dos." Why? Have you had the experience of working for 12 hours and crossing off 10 to 20 to-dos things on your list, but at the end of the day still feel unfulfilled? I bet the answer is yes, and this is precisely what we are trying to avoid.

My view of time management and being busy was shifted by Derek Sivers, a successful and low-key entrepreneur and investor, who said, "Every time people contact me, they say, 'Look, I know you must be incredibly busy' and I always think, 'No, I'm not.' Because I'm in control of my time. I'm on top of it. **Busy to me, seems to imply out of control.** Like, 'Oh my God, I'm so busy. I don't have any time for this shit!' To me, that sounds like a person who's got no control over their life."

Tim Ferriss, a famous author, entrepreneur, and productivity expert agrees. Tim has famously said that, "**Lack of time is actually lack of priorities.**"[2] If I'm "busy," it is because I've made choices that put me in that position, so I've forbidden myself to reply to "How are you?" with "Busy." **I have no right to complain.**

## RPM METHOD

Stop thinking about "What do I need to do?" RPM is a system developed by Tony Robbins after he went through most of the popular time management systems and found that they did not deliver on their promise. Many people I know agree with me that RPM is one of the best tools we know and use.

The first step toward taking back your focus and achieving the realization of your vision is to **ask yourself three questions in a specific sequence** on a consistent basis, the **RPM** system.

Although RPM stands for the *Rapid Planning Method*, you can also think of it as a **Results-oriented/Purpose-driven/ Massive Action Plan.** The sequence is critical because **if you don't know what you want, why you want it, and *then* create a plan for how to get to it, in that order, you are significantly less likely to accomplish your plans.**

- **Result:** Before you can answer the question, "What am I going to do?" you've got to first ask the question, "What do I want?" That shift in focus will change completely how you respond in your life. It will change your focus from everyone else's demands for your attention, or what you're afraid of, or what might give you pleasure in the moment, to what's most important to you.

- **Purpose:** The fuel behind getting there is having a compelling purpose and a reason that will move you. This fuel is the thing that will carry you through hard times without giving up. What are my reasons? Why is this not just a "should," but a *must* for me? The *emotional quality* of purpose makes what you will do not only sustainable, but *powerful*.

- **Massive action plan**: Now it is time to create your action plan and make things happen. One useful tool is chunking. It is overwhelming to have 20 things on your to-do list. Look at your list and chunk similar activities into fewer categories (or outcomes) to help the brain process. For example, homework, office hours, and group projects can be chunked as school work. Cook dinner, workout, and grocery shopping can be chunked as physical health. In addition, once you create your list of actions, it is helpful to schedule the items into your calendar.[3]

## THE ONE THING METHOD

Another helpful tool I discovered is the "One Thing Method" by productivity expert Tim Ferriss.

"Personally," Tim said, "I suck at efficiency (doing things quickly). To compensate and cope, here's my process for maximizing efficacy (doing the right things to produce a desired or intended result)." (Note that I've simplified this process for you):

- Wake up at least one hour before you have to be at a computer screen. Email is a mind-killer.
- Write down 3 or 5 things—and no more—that are making you the most anxious or uncomfortable. They're often things that have been punted from one day's to-do list to the next, to the next, and so on. "Most important" usually equals "most uncomfortable," with some chance of rejection or conflict.
- For each item, ask yourself the following questions:
- "If this were the only thing I accomplished today, would I be satisfied with my day?"
  - "Will moving this forward make all the other to-dos unimportant or easier to knock off later?"
  - "What, if this is done, will it make all of the rest of my list easier or irrelevant?"
  - Then focus only on the items you've answered "yes" to—for at least one of these questions.
- Block out at least two hours to focus on ONE of those items today. Let the rest of the urgent, but less important stuff slide. It will still be there tomorrow. TO BE CLEAR: this is ONE BLOCK OF TIME. Cobbling together 10 minutes here and there to add up to 120 minutes does not work. No phone calls or social media allowed.
- If you get distracted or start procrastinating, don't freak out and downward-spiral; just gently come back to your ONE to-do.3

Congratulations! That's it. This is the only way I can create big outcomes despite my never-ending impulse to procrastinate, nap, and otherwise fritter away days with bullshit. If I have ten important things to do in a day, it's 100% certain nothing important will get done that day. On the other hand, I can usually handle one must-do item and block out my less effective behaviors for two hours a day. It doesn't take much to seem superhuman and appear "successful" to nearly everyone around you. In fact, you just need one rule: **What you do is more important than how you do it.**"[4]

## ACTION CHECKLIST

- ☐ Use RPM to determine your desired outcomes. Apply this to your daily schedule for a week.
- ☐ Start to track how you spend your time every hour for a week. Evaluate at the end.
- ☐ Experiment with the "One Thing" exercise by Tim Ferriss for 3-5 days.

## CHAPTER 18

# THE IN-DEMAND SUPERPOWER: DEEP WORK

———

*"The ability to perform deep work is becoming increasingly rare at exactly the same time it is becoming increasingly valuable in our economy. As a consequence, the few who cultivate this skill, and then make it the core of their working life, will thrive."*

— CAL NEWPORT

*"I'll live the focused life, because it's the best kind there is."*

— WINIFRED FALLAGHER

Did you know humans now have shorter attention span than the notoriously ill-focused goldfish according to a new study from Microsoft Corp?[1] This tragedy is mostly caused by the effect of an increasingly digitized lifestyle on the brain. This 2015 research was shocking but not surprising to me. Why? Because I have had many personal experiences when my attention span felt shorter than that of a goldfish. I find it hard to focus, especially when tempted by technologies and social media outlets. In general, I am one of those people who suffer from an extremely active mind. For the most part, that enables me to actually focus only when I am working on a deadline, which is not a healthy way of living.

As a matter of fact, to get myself focused, I deleted all the social media apps on my phone for the last couple intense days spent writing this book. I did not go so far as deactivating my Facebook page, but I came pretty close. Why? I was in a desperate frenzy to focus and get work done. In short, I wanted the power to concentrate, a skill the author Cal Newport would describe as a superpower. Cal's latest book is titled *Deep Work: Rules for Focused Success in a Distracted World,* which I highly recommend. Fun fact, "deleting social media from your cellphone" was the advice Prof. Newport gave me at the end of our interview. And, boy, I am happy that I followed his advice!

Deep Work means professional activities performed in a state of distraction-free concentration that pushes your cognitive capabilities to their limit. On the other hand, Shallow Work is non-cognitively demanding logistical-style tasks, often performed while distracted. These efforts tend to not create much new value in the world and are easy to replicate.[2]

The two main benefits of deep work that are particularly important in this new technological age and in entrepreneurship are: **1. Quickly mastering difficult topics or skills and, 2. Producing at an elite level in both quality and speed.**[3]

**Deep work is Valuable, Rare, and Meaningful.** Prof. Newport discovered that when you study the lives of influential figures from both distant and recent history, you will find a commitment to deep work common there. Mark Twain wrote much of *The Adventure of Tom Sawyer* in a shed on a remote farm where he was spending the summer. Twain's study was so isolated from the main house that his family took to blowing a horn to attract his attention. Peter Higgs, a theoretical physicist who also rejects computers, performs his work in such disconnected isolation that journalists couldn't find him after it was announced that he won the Nobel Prize. J.K Rowling, on the other hand, does use a computer, but was conspicuously absent from social media during the writing of Harry Potter.

The same applies in the business world. Microsoft CEO Bill Gates famously conducted "Think Weeks" twice a year, during which he would isolate himself (often in a lakeside cottage) to do nothing but read and think big thoughts. Many other famous entrepreneurs such as Mark Zuckerberg and Mark Cuban reportedly have long periods of time of intense focus, even forgetting to eat or sleep. Zuckerberg reportedly could work for more than 20 hours without stopping because he was so immersed in writing code in his dorm room.

During my interview with Cal, we put deep work into the framework of education entrepreneurship. He said, "I mean, it's a very fundamental skill for education. You can learn things quickly and get deeper insights. You can produce better stuff in less time. It's like a magic formula." The same thing applies to entrepreneurship, if you want to be great at something or create meaningful work or a good product, deep work is required.

Cal continued saying, "It's basically like a professional athlete who trains really hard in the weight room. The training in the weight room makes their baseball season better, football season better, basketball season better. This is the weight room for being a college student. You might have trained your ability to concentrate while most other students are really bad at it, so then that means you have a huge advantage. It's like being in a sport and you're the only one who knows about the weight room."

## CULTIVATING YOUR ABILITY TO DO DEEP WORK

The good news is this ability to concentrate and do deep work can be learned. This could also be bad news for people because it takes time to develop. "People get this wrong because they think about the ability to concentrate is like flossing. They know how to do it, and they just probably need to put aside more time for it. But in fact, it's a skill like playing the guitar: if you don't practice it you're not going to be good at it," Cal said.

## PRACTICING DEEP WORK

### FIRST: RITUALIZE DEEP WORK

- **When**: Devote at least two hours (as one chunk) in your daily schedule for deep work. Preferably the time is fairly consistent so your brain gets used to it
- **Where**: Ritual needs a specialized location. It could be a usual workplace, or you can pick a place for deep work only.
- **How**: Rules and processes can help structure your ritual. Set up rules around Internet use and outcome measurement such as word count and pages read.
- **Support**: This can include coffee, the right type of food, light exercises. Support can also be environmental, such as having all the necessary materials

## FOUR DISCIPLINES OF EXECUTION (FROM HBS PROFESSOR CHRISTENSEN)

- Focus on the Wildly Important (It's more about what you do, not how you do it)
- Act on the Lead Measures
    - lag measures (usually means the results) are too late
    - lead measure for deep work: time spent in deep work dedicated toward your wildly important goal
- Keep a compelling Scoreboard
    - track hours of deep work in a prominent place
- Create a Cadence of Accountability (regular progress reports)

## BE LAZY

- Downtime aids insights
- Downtime helps recharge the energy needed to work deeply
- The work that evening downtime replaces is usually not that important

Working deeply does not necessarily mean working in isolation

## SECOND: EMBRACE BOREDOM

This rule will significantly help you to improve your current limit of concentration ability and overcome your desire for distraction.

I did not quite understand it, so Cal explained to me, "In most people, we build up this connection that, 'every time I'm bored I get a quick distraction.' You know: 'I'm in line and waiting for something, I pull up the phone.' **The issue is when it comes time to do deep work, your mind just doesn't tolerate it because deep work is boring in the sense that you don't have a lot of new stimuli.** So, if every single time your mind gets bored it gets stimulated, then it's not going to tolerate keeping on working. Therefore, you actually have to have a lot more boredom in your life, so that when it comes time to do deep work, your mind is capable of doing it."

Cal recommends scheduling time for using the Internet and social media. Schedule blocks of time; even if your work requires a lot of online work use, you can create blocks, such as 15 minutes per hour. Block yourself from using the Internet outside of the blocks.

## THIRD: QUIT SOCIAL MEDIA (OR JUST TAKE IT OFF YOUR PHONE!)

I think I don't need to reiterate the negatively addictive effects of social media here.

Cal recommended to me to take all the social media applications off my phone because these apps are engineered to have an addictive business model, so that you'll look at it often. I was happy to hear this because limiting access to the web seems to be a more reasonable alternative than quitting social media altogether. One of the main reasons I do rely on Facebook is that this is the best way to keep in touch with many of my friends who live outside of the country.

## DRAIN THE SHALLOWS

- Schedule every minute of your day. Most people spend their time on autopilot, studies show that people drastically over-estimate the time they work and underestimate the time they play (or watch TV).
- The goal of a schedule is not to force behavior into a rigid plan, but to make you more thoughtful. Track your time. Quantify the depth of each activity.
- Finish work by 5:30 pm. Stop saying you can't. Instead, focus on improving productivity through deep work, rather than adding hours and hours of shallow work to your workday[4]

Prof. Newport had some beautiful closing words.

"The deep life, of course, is not for everybody. It requires hard work and drastic change to your habits. For many, there is a comfort in the artificial business of rapid e-mail messaging and social media posturing, while a deep life requires you to leave much of that behind. There is also an uneasiness that surrounds any effort to produce the best things you are capable of producing, as this force confronts the possibility that your best is not (yet) that good."

"But if you are willing to sidestep your comforts and fears, and instead struggle to employ your mind to its fullest capacity to create things that matter, then you will discover, as many others have before you, that depth generates a life rich with productivity and meaning. As I quoted writer Winifred Fallagher saying, 'I'll live the focused life, because it's the best kind there is.' "[4]

I agree. So does Bill Gates. And hopefully after finishing this chapter, you do too.

## ACTION CHECKLIST

☐ Consider your life goals and how you would benefit from creating a deep work ritual.

☐ Experiment for a week with the following:

   ☐ Finish work before 8pm everyday

   ☐ Go to bed at 10pm

   ☐ Wake up at 6 am

   ☐ Devote 3-4 hours to deep work

CHAPTER 19

# HOW TO HACK
# COLLEGE

———

*Intelligence without ambition is like birds without wings.*

— SALVADOR DALI

What does it take to be a standout student? How can you make the most of your college years—graduate with honors, choose exciting activities, build a head-turning resume, and gain access to the best post-college opportunities? Based on interviews with star students at universities nationwide, from Harvard to the University of Arizona, Cal Newport wrote *How to Win at College: Surprising Secrets for Success from the Country's Top Students*, a book that presents seventy-five simple rules that will rocket you to a fantastic college experience.

Below are my favorite points from Cal Newport's book with some of my additions. I highly recommend his book to all of you.

## DON'T DO ALL YOUR READING

For reading that covers the topic of an upcoming lecture, it's often sufficient just to skim the main points ahead of time and then fill in the gaps during class by taking good notes. Students are sometimes afraid of skimming, but you shouldn't be. You need to master the skill of covering hundreds of pages of text very quickly. The secret is to read chapter introductions and conclusions carefully, and then skim everything else. Make tick marks next to sentences that catch your attention, as this is faster than highlighting.

## BECOME A CLUB PRESIDENT

It is a lot more manageable than most students think. And it is one of the best ways to improve your leadership and inter-personal skills. It looks good on a resume too.

## SEEK OUT PHENOMENAL ACHIEVERS

Find the extraordinary people on campus and connect with them. The term "achievers" is relative to each person. They can be Rhodes Scholars, Nobel Laureates, the professor who wrote your textbook, students who started companies or organizations, or a quiet drama major who has won a bevy of creative awards. Find these people. Meet them. Treat them to a meal, and let them spill their guts to you. Find out how they did what they did, what it felt like, and what are they up to next. There are many benefits to doing this. To expose yourself to possibilities, expand your network, and gain a different perspective. And to a people person like me, I feel a charge of energy when I talk with people who have done amazing things because I sense a pull to raise my standards.

## NEVER PULL AN ALL-NIGHTER

Just don't do it. You will find countless studies on how bad it is for your health and productivity. If you allocated your studies properly, you shouldn't ever need to do an all-nighter. If you do need to do some emergency work, at least sleep couple hours. And the best ROI on sleep is found by researchers if you fall asleep before midnight. So sleep from 10pm-2am will recharge your body more effectively than 4am-8am.

## ASK ONE QUESTION AT EACH LECTURE

This is a simple strategy to make sure you pay attention to the professor *and* the professor pays attention to you. By the way, talking while having the entire class staring at you is also effective to wake you up if you feel sleepy. (I'm not indicating that you ever felt sleepy in class at all.)


## ALWAYS SIT IN THE FIRST ROW

One day in my junior year, I realized that this might be the single most significant factor that saved my grades from my crazy traveling and activities. Ching, a friend of mine, gave me this advice before I started college. Ching graduated from Hong Kong Polytechnic University as the valedictorian and then went on to get a Ph.D. from MIT while earning multiple patents. I simply acted on his advice. This rule is great because it forces you to pay attention in class, and you automatically receive the cognitive bias most professors have for the "front-row students."


## DON'T STUDY IN YOUR ROOM

Based on personal experience, this one is much harder to do than I expected. Many times I just feel too lazy to study in the library, but the low productivity is embarrassing. If you want to take this to another level, only study in libraries because the study atmosphere is stronger in a library than other parts of a school. And you will get more done just by being in that atmosphere.

## STUDY ABROAD

When would you get to spend months living in a different country with different culture and language? College is the most likely the time in your life that you will get to do this. Studying abroad is a beautiful experience. Even though I spent a semester abroad, I regret not spending two semesters away. This an adjustment I would make if I get to do college again. Also, a couple of founders including Aaron Rasmussen and Nathan Chan also recommended studying abroad and traveling as a way of gaining different perspectives.

## BEFRIEND A PROFESSOR

Most professors want to engage and help the students. Some professors are successful and fascinating human beings. While this is a great way to get more recommendation letters, it will also make your college experience that much more personal and enjoyable. How do you befriend professors? Go talk to them during office hours, propose a coffee meeting, discuss things outside of classes, and most importantly, actually be curious about them and their work.

## SCHEDULE EVERYTHING

Use college as an excellent way to practice juggling multiple things at the same time by managing your time well. The best way I have found is to schedule everything, including time to study, hanging out with friends, working out, grocery shopping, etc. In other words, get in the habit of putting events on a calendar versus trying to "remember." This way, you are less likely to fail to do the things you intended to do or get overwhelmed by too many moving pieces. This habit is beneficial in the professional world as well.

## MAKE YOUR FRIENDS YOUR NO. 1 PRIORITY

If you are already in college, you probably realized that spending quality time with friends is actually not an easy thing to do because of the other millions of things you need to do. This is just a friendly reminder that people and friends are the most important part of college and life in general. Schedule enough time to create some magical moments together.

## LEARN IMPORTANT THINGS
## OUTSIDE OF CLASSROOMS

As I mentioned in earlier parts of the book, what you can learn from classes is very limited, but the free time in college is plenty. If you put in the time and work to become great at something you care about, this could be a key that can open many doors for you after graduation.

## PICK PROFESSORS OVER CLASSES

Look for great professors rather than interesting course titles because great professors are more likely to impact the way you think and learn. Also, their passion will help you engage more with the classes. I have made multiple mistakes where I chose interesting class titles over professors, and I have regretted all those decisions.

## ACTION CHECKLIST

☐ Make a list of ways you can apply all the points above.

☐ Make a list of people you can spend time with and brainstorm questions to ask them.

☐ Come up with fun ideas to spend time with your friends.

## CHAPTER 20

# LEARN ANYTHING FASTER

---

*"It is possible to become world-class, enter the top 5% of performers in the world, in almost any subject within 6-12 months, or even 6-12 weeks."*

— TIMOTHY FERRISS

*"During finals, I would go to the library to make my friends feel better. (Even though I didn't need to cram)."*

— CAL NEWPORT

When was the last time you examined how you read and tried to improve it? If you are like most people, that was probably in elementary school. When I thought about this, I thought, "Isn't this crazy?" Students spend the majority of their time reading. Yet, most people never tried to improve their reading. Maybe this idea has never crossed your mind before, but with your newfound optimization mindset, you shouldn't be surprised that we are hacking learning here.

You can cut your study time by 50% and get better grades! I won't list out specific techniques for you in this chapter because I know you can find them online or at your college's tutoring center. Instead, I will share some of my favorite tips and resources on accelerated learning.

My favorites:

1. Two things to focus on when starting to hack learning: reading and memory. These are the two areas that will give you the highest ROI (return on investment).

2. The simplest way to increase learning efficiency is to have clear outcomes. That is, being clear about what you want to know from an article or book will turn on your brain to find relevant information.

3. Help your brain by always going from big picture to details. For example, when you read a book, look at the table of contents to get a general idea about the book, then read the section headline of each chapter, then read the chapter.

4. The more senses you engage while learning, the better you will learn.

5. Active learning is significantly more effective than passive

learning (even though we have been trained to learn passively since we were young).

6. Having a routine study system is important. Systemize what you need to study and how. Create checklists and routines. You can ask your professor or the tutoring center for help with this.

7. The emotional state you are in while learning something will be linked to the content you learn. You are more likely to use the information you learned in an excited or happy state, rather than in a bored or indifferent state. So, get yourself interested and excited while learning whenever you can. (reference the chapter on "beautiful state)

8. Tim Ferriss's four-step "DiSSS" system (read more in his book *Four-Hour Chef*).

    ♦ Deconstruction: "What are the minimal learnable units, the LEGO blocks, I should be starting with?"

    ♦ Selection: "Which 20% of the blocks should I focus on for 80% (or more) of the outcome I want?"

    ♦ Sequencing: "In what order should I learn the blocks?"

    ♦ Stakes: "How do I set up stakes to create real consequences and guarantee I follow the program?"

## RESOURCES:

### BOOKS

1. *Four-Hour Chef: The Simple Path to Cooking Like a Pro, Learning Anything, and Living the Good Life* by Tim Ferriss (A must read!

I promise it's not just a cookbook. On the other hand, knowing how to cook is good for your well-being!)

2. *How to Become a Straight-A Student: The Unconventional Strategies Real College Students Use to Score High While Studying Less* by Cal Newport

3. *Moonwalking with Einstein: The Art and Science of Remembering Everything* by Joshua Foer

4. *Thinking, Fast and Slow* by Daniel Kahneman

5. *The Talent Code: Greatness Isn't Born. It's Grown. Here's How* by Daniel Coyle

6. *Unlimited Memory: How to Use Advanced Learning Strategies to Learn Faster, Remember More and be More Productive* by Kevin Horsley

7. *Speed Reading: How to Double (or Triple) Your Reading Speed in Just 1 Hour!* by Justin Hammond

8. *Photoreading: Read with Greater Speed, Comprehension, and Enjoyment to Absorb Complete Books in Minutes* by Paul Scheele (This book is a little out there, but it's a good try if you are bored with the traditional speed reading methods.)

## VIDEOS

1. "Tim Ferriss shares how to master any skill by deconstructing it" (Tim Ferriss)

2. "How to Learn Anything...Fast" by Josh Kaufman

3. "Study Less Study Smart" by Marty Lobdell

4. "What Do Top Students Do Differently?" by Douglas Barton

5. "SuperheroYou: Memory Part 1 (Remembering Names & Faces)" by Jim Kwik
6. "How to Triple Your Reading Speed in 20 Minutes" by Tim Ferriss
7. "Tim Ferriss Teaches Speed Reading" by Tim Ferriss

## GOOGLE THE FOLLOWING:

1. How to double your reading speed in 20 mins
2. Accelerate learning tips
3. How to improve your memory
4. Jim Kwik ( Jim is the founder of Kwik Learning, and he is arguably the most famous person in the field of accelerated learning)
5. Tim Ferriss on accelerated learning

## ACTION CHECKLIST

☐ Purchase 3 books from the recommended list today.

☐ Watch at least 1 recommended video today.

☐ Create a plan to develop your accelerated learning skills.

☐ Plan to spend at least 30 minutes every day on improving yourself by reading or watching videos.

## CHAPTER 21

# DANCE WITH FEAR

—

*"Fear has two meanings. Forget everything and run or face everything and rise. The choice is yours."*

— ZIG ZIGLAR

*"Life is the dance between your greatest desires and deepest fears."*

— TONY ROBBINS

I was standing barefoot in a parking lot. In front of me was an eight-foot strip of burning hot coals around 1000 degrees Fahrenheit. There were 8000 other people surrounding me who were also doing the firewalk from the "Unleash the Power Within" seminar with Tony Robbins. My heart was racing, and my stomach was hurting a little, from both nervousness and hunger. Despite the training and preparation we did for hours in the seminar, I started to doubt myself. **"For God's**

**sake, it's freaking burning coals!"** Then I heard the trainer ask, "Ready?" It seemed too late to back out. I distinctly remember the moment I made the decision to go. It seemed like time stopped. "Screw it. Let's do this!"

I walked. I walked fast using all the techniques taught to us to ensure safety. My eyes were focused on the other side. Yes, I could feel the hot coals, really hot. Then it was over. Someone splashed some water on my feet for safety. I thought to myself, "That's it! I did it!" Instead of an urge to jump up and down and celebrate like most people did, I felt relieved and empowered. I thought to myself, "That was not as bad as I thought at all." I guess people are right when they say "The only thing that keeps you from moving forward is fear." We make up fear in our minds, sometimes we allow it to grow irrationally overwhelming to the point of making us feel powerless. **However, the only person that can overcome your fear is you, and the best way to overcome fear is to do precisely what scares you the most. Afterwards, you will feel on top of the world.**

**"The only thing that is keeping anyone from starting a company is the fear of failure,"** said Bill Carmody, a founder of an advertising agency and contributor to *Inc.* magazine. This is one of the highlights of the interview for me. Bill went on to explain, "Now is the best time to start a company. The barrier to entry is so low because of the great presence of the Internet and social media marketing. You can spend 30 minutes to create an ad and landing page. And spend five dollars on Facebook to test if real customers are willing to pay for what you offer. This kind of low barrier to entry never existed before."

**Fear is the number one factor that stops us from moving forward, but fear is natural.** Fear is here to keep us safe, but it does not want us to change or grow. The first step in the dance with fear is to be aware of it. Start to be aware and curious. When you sense a resistance to doing something, ask yourself what the fear behind it is. For example, I spent days trying to distract myself from writing by watching TV, doing research, or other small tasks. I leaned on excuses such as: "I don't feel like writing," or "I need more research," and "I need to interview more people." But in the end, I realized that it was my fear of failure holding me back, the fear of failing to write the perfect chapter. This fear kept me from writing altogether. When you want to reach out to a potential client, a potential mentor, or anyone in a position of power, if you hesitate, the fear of rejection is probably at play. In the case of a startup, I can find millions of reasons for not starting a company: "we don't have the right team," or "the product is not good enough," or "the economy is not good," and the list goes on. **The key is to be able to tell the difference between your fear of failure and actual concerns.** Once you are aware of the fear you are experiencing, you have completed half the battle. **By being aware of your fear, for most situations, you will start to see how irrational the fears are.**

**Remember, fear is just an emotional state, so are confidence, happiness, certainty.** As as you learned in the "Lead Your Own Ship" chapter, you can change your state instantly.

**Once you are in a positive state, proceed to "fear setting,"** a technique developed by best-selling author and lifestyle entrepreneur Tim Ferriss. Tim believes that people typically don't overcome their fears because the fears are nebulous and undefined.[1] To get over them then, you need to drag your fears out into the open and confront them.

Begin by thinking of a goal that is important to you but that you've kept yourself from striving for. Then divide a piece of paper into three columns.

- In the first column, write down all of the things that could go wrong should your attempt fail. Think of the most terrible things possible.
- In the second column, determine ways that you can mitigate the possibility of each of those bad consequences from happening.
- In the third column, think of how you would recover from each of the scenarios you imagined in the first column.

| ALL THE THINGS THAT COULD GO WRONG | ACTIONS TO MITIGATE THE POSSIBILITIES | ACTIONS TO RECOVER FROM THE BAD SCENARIOS |
|---|---|---|
| | | |

"You come away from that exercise realizing, 'Wow, I was getting extremely anxious and all worked up over something that is completely preventable, reversible, or just not a very big deal,'" Tim says.

In addition, to help people deal with common fears such as fear of failure, rejection, or being judged, Tim has created many "Comfort Challenges." This is the act of performing an uncomfortable task for the sole purpose of overcoming the fear associated with it. These challenges are one of the best ways to stretch your comfort zone and live life the way you've always dreamed of living it. Tim says, "They've shown me that the only person truly in charge of my life is myself. Use comfort challenges to free yourself from the constraints of your mind, and to prove to yourself that you can have anything you want in life, if you are willing to go after it."[2]

Here's a short list of exercises to help expand your comfort zone:

- **Give a Compliment to a Stranger**

  This seems to be an easy thing to do, and it could be. But sometimes I still find myself hesitating to give a compliment due to irrational fear such as "it might look weird."

- **Maintain Eye Contact**

  The next time you are in public, pick a stranger and lock eyes with him or her. The initial response when your eyes meet will be to look away. Maintain eye contact until he or she breaks it first.

- **Ask For a 10% Discount**

  The next time you pay for a coffee, ice cream, or tea, ask the cashier for a 10% discount off your purchase. Don't give a reason, just ask.

- **Tell a Corny Joke to a Stranger**

  Pick a stranger on the street, go up to him, and tell him a short, corny joke.

- **Lie Down In Public**

  Once you get more comfortable with the easier challenges, give this one a try. Go to a crowded area, like a farmers market or Starbucks, and lie down on the floor for 10 seconds.

- **Ask a Stranger for His or Her Number**

  This one takes a lot of guts, especially if the other person is opposite gender.

After working with millions of people across the globe, Tony Robbins says that our deepest fear is, "If I am not enough, I won't be loved." Tony believes if you keep digging into people's fears, you will find this is the deepest fear we all share. Just as Oprah once shared the one question that every guest asked her after interviewing, "Did I do ok?" Oprah said that this question is the "common denominator" for all her guests no matter who they are. You can also reflect on your experiences and see if it's true.

We all want to be enough and to be loved. Know that it's normal to feel "not good enough." Even the most successful and iconic people in the world share this fear. Be kind to yourself and others. Just don't let the fear keep you from moving forward. Remember: courage is not a lack of fear; courage is being scared but taking the action anyways.

## ACTION CHECKLIST

- ☐ Start to observe and be aware of your fears.
- ☐ Write down a big goal and apply the fear setting exercises.
- ☐ Do at least one comfort challenge once a week.

# CHAPTER 22

# STARTUP 101

___

*"The only way to win is to learn faster than anyone else."*

— ERIC RIES

*"We must learn what customers really want, not what they say they want or what we think they should want."*

— ERIC RIES

Remember that No.1 cause for startup failure is building something nobody wants? This single factor causes 36% of startups go out of business. In this chapter, we will hack this problem because it ties into many other important parts of starting a company. In the process of making something people want, the startup needs to do market research, connect with customers, design tests, launch minimal viable products, collect customer feedback, make adjustments. For a more thorough guide on starting a company, check out the book *Lean Startup* by Eric Ries.

How do you build something people want?

1.   Make sure the problem is the right one. Some people get distracted by the surface problem versus the root cause.
2.   Validate that enough people actually care about the problem you are trying to solve. This is not lip service. Most people will tell you nice things when you ask for opinions. So, seeing enough real customers willing to *pay money* to get this problem solved is crucial.
3.   Create a solution, in the form of a Minimum Viable Product (MVP). So that you test important assumptions, learn fast based on customer feedback, and adjust your product, which will lead to creating something people want.

## HOW TO BUILD AND USE A MINIMUM VIABLE PRODUCT

The wrong way to launch is to spend too much time planning and building your product without any customers. The right way to launch is to get out a Minimum Viable Product so you can earn and learn as soon as possible.

Eric explains, "A Minimum Viable Product is that version of a new product which allows a team to collect the maximum amount of validated learning about customers with the least effort."

How to create an MVP in the fastest time possible:

- Define who your ideal customer is.
- Focus on the problem you're going to solve for them.
- Create a solution with the minimum number of steps to results.

Collect a small number of beta users, and launch your MVP to your beta group to test and measure:

- How happy are they when they use it?
- How often do they continue to use it?
- How many others do they refer the product to?

Then create a version 2, 3, 4 based on what you learn and what they tell you:

- What would make the product even better?
- What are they willing to pay for?
- How much are they willing to pay?

An MVP isn't about getting your ideal product, but getting your ideal customer, and then co-creating the next version from their feedback. If in doubt, if you're ready to launch, then launch first and check later.[1]

## THE KEY: PIVOTING WITH CUSTOMER FEEDBACK

One of the most important foundations to building a successful company is to pivot or change based on customer feedback and insight. There is a misconception that a company just comes out of nowhere and rides the founder's brilliant idea to take over the world. **In reality, most companies don't execute a single brilliant master plan. They go through stops and starts, a couple near-death experiences, and a great deal of adaptation.**

Pixar started as a company that sold a special computer for doing digital animation; it took a while for them to get into the moviemaking business. Similarly, Starbucks originally sold only coffee beans and coffee equipment; they hadn't planned to sell coffee by the cup.

Airbnb started as an air mattress and breakfast provider for big conventions and conferences. The founders did not even consider the possibility of extending Airbnb outside of the convention space because they did not see a demand. Airbnb started because the founders realized that, for some big conventions, the demand for accommodations and hotels far exceeded the supply of hotel rooms. Then they started to change their business models and plans to expand their business after receiving many user requests for their service at the places the customers travelled to. Along the way, they also chose to pivot away from the "air mattress only" rule.

Another example is Instagram. Kevin Systrom, the co-founder of Instagram, worked on another app called Burbn, an HTML5 check-in service, before he started Instagram. However, Burbn was not taking off at all. Systrom was frustrated. He and his group started to dig for some customer insight trying to identify why the people who continued to use the service kept using it. When they looked at their user base, their whole customer base loved the photo aspect much more than the other 10+ features. So they made a change and ended up focusing on photos. But there were already a bunch of photo websites and even photo apps. Systrom worried about how they would be able to come up with an idea that would make their app different.

Systrom got a little sick, so he and his wife took a break to Mexico. While having a conversation with his wife about a photo sharing feature, Kevin's wife liked the idea, but said she probably wouldn't post that many pictures. Systrom asked why, and his wife explained it was because her photos do not look as good as her friends' did. Systrom tried to make his wife feel better by explaining that many of her friends use filters to make the pictures look good. It was that moment in which Systrom discovered something that could differentiate them from the other competitors, and the rest is history.

## ACTION CHECKLIST

☐ Look for problems people are willing to pay to get solved.

☐ Test assumptions using MVP guidelines.

☐ Adjust or pivot based on customer feedback.

# ATTRACTION AND PERSUASION

———

*Marketing is getting the right message to the right people via the right media and methods."*

— DAN KENNEDY

*"In its purest sense marketing is a combination of educating someone on the advantages you offer or your product or service offers and increasing their demand or desire to get those benefits from you and no one else."*

— JAY ABRAHAM

Influence and persuasion is a fancier way of explaining marketing and sales. I asked every entrepreneur I interviewed the question "What should entrepreneurial students learn?" Marketing and sales are always the first or second thing they mention.

## MARKETING

The first part of marketing has nothing to do with communications or ads or messages. It has to do with the concept of the product or service itself. How well the product is designed to solve the problems of a specific target market. In *Purple Cow: Transform Your Business by Being Remarkable*, Seth Godin wrote, "Start with a problem you can solve for the customers." In other words, marketing is not something you do after you create the product; the fact that most marketing is done this way is why we hate the word "marketing" so much. **If you start with marketing—that is, with thinking about, anticipating, and meeting the needs of a market in an original, effective, compelling way—then that market will be glad to hear about what you're offering.**[1]

While designing your solution or product, it is crucial to create something different than other offerings on the market. **Differentiation or Unique Selling Point (USP) is key.** USP is the one thing your business does differently—and preferably better—than anybody else. Maybe it's reliable post-purchase service, super-human delivery speeds, or round-the-clock client service. It could even be your convenient location. Whatever it is, your UPS is the single most valuable asset you possess as a business owner. It's the engine that's going to drive your success. After defining a USP, then you should mention and promote the USP as much as possible.[2] In the best case, your USP becomes so remarkable that people start to talk about it. Creating something remarkable is the best way for a company to grow and market. The main idea beyond Seth's book *Purple Cow* is that you need to work super hard to market regular cows because the differentiation is small. This explains why we hate boring marketing trying to convince us to buy a new brand of toothpaste. However, if you had a purple cow, it is so remarkable that people will talk about it and drive 100 miles to see it.

Once you have a unique product, it's time to let people know about it. The key to promotion is creating messages that customers care about. No one cares about the product and specific features other than the seller. **Customers care about the benefits they can gain from the product or features.** The more you can tie the benefits into emotions the better. A good tool to help you accomplish this is empathy. Seth Godin believes that empathy is hard because it involves trying to feel the way others feel. Empathy challenges you to set aside your comfortable, familiar worldview in exchange for a perspective that may feel awkwardly foreign. It's hard because it requires you to imagine what you do not know. **The perspectives of the people you wish to change will shape how they digest the marketing you present to them.** What these people believe in, what worries them, what excites them, and what they desire will influence their decisions far more than any stack of statistics you pitch to them. **Once you start to understand how these people think, you'll know how to *talk with* them, rather than *market at* them.** By showing that you understand their needs and hopes, you are much likelier to earn their attention and trust in your ability to fulfill your promises.

Lastly, it's about getting the message to the right target audiences via the right channels. Rather than the mass media channels—such as TV, billboards, and newspapers—digital marketing medias—such as AdWords and paid media on social media platforms—allow you to target people a lot more precisely. On some digital marketing platforms, you can target people by demographics, psychographics, geography, interests, schools, employers, and many other ways.

Remember that power of testing can and should be applied in marketing as well. Identify the appropriate metrics, such as cost per impression, cost per click, cost per acquisition, conversation rate, etc. Then always be testing the target audiences, ad image, ad copy, and more. Learning fast is a key component to success in today's marketing world.

## SALES

People buy what they want, not what they need. Think about

three recent purchases you made, what percentage of the decision is influenced by emotions versus logic? If you are like most people, emotion would probably be 80% and logic would be 20%. In most cases, we make emotional reasons to buy because the purchase makes us feel a certain way, then we justify it with logic. And if our emotional reasons to buy plus logical reasons to buy outweigh our dominant reason to avoid buying (time, price, complexity, social pressure, etc.), we make the decision to buy and vice versa.

Emotional reasons to buy (ERTB) + Logical reasons to buy (LRTB) > Dominant reason to avoid buying (GRAG)

How do you find out the ERTB, LRTB, and DRAG of the customer you want to influence? The answer is to **listen**. My interviewers with experts revealed that listening is believed to be the most important yet overlooked factor for successful sales. People will tell you what they want, what they fear, and their objections, if you listen carefully. Further, people want to be understood and not sold to, which connects back to listening. If you were trying to buy a car, would you buy from someone who just tells you about the car features or from someone who tries to understand your needs by listening to you? Simple choice right? When your intention is to understand and help the customers is added to your passion in your product and knowledge about competitors, you are much more likely to create a successful sale.

The ultimate goal of both marketing and sales is to become the trusted advisor for customers. As marketing expert Jay Abraham says, "People are silently begging to be led. They're crying out to know more about your product/service. Educate them."[2] When we face a major purchasing decision, we want people who are knowledgeable in that field for advice. This is what Jay means by being the advisor. At the same time, we normally turn to friends and families for advice because we trust them and we know they want the best for us. This is what Jay calls "trusted." We all want to turn to knowledgeable advisors who have our best interests in mind for help. No one wants to do tedious research and decision-making process if we can just ask for advice from a trusted advisor. As an entrepreneur, this means to create a product or service that is genuinely better in some ways and align with customer's interest. Then establish yourself as an expert in the field by producing relevant content and creating good results.

## ACTION CHECKLIST

☐ Learn more about marketing and sales every week.

☐ Check out works of Seth Godin, Jay Abraham, and Harvey MacKay. Find other experts to learn from based on your own research.

☐ Take on a marketing or sales role in a student organization or an internship

CHAPTER 24

# RESOURCES TO STAY ON THE EDGE OF THE ENTREPRENEURIAL WORLD

———

*"Stay hungry, stay foolish."*

— STEVE JOBS

*"I see life like one long university education that I never had. Every day I'm learning something new."*

— RICHARD BRANSON

This is a chapter of lists, most of which are from *Entrepreneur Inspiration* created by Roger Hamilton, an incredible resource filled with fun stories and insights.[1] Roger is a world-renowned futurist and social entrepreneur, and he is the Founder of the Entrepreneurs Institute and the creator of GeniusU, Wealth Dynamics & Talent Dynamics, used by over 700,000 entrepreneurs to follow their flow. I also added the most helpful resources I have encountered along the way.

This chapter has four parts:
- People to Follow on Social Media
- Distilled Wisdom
- Must-Read Books
- Podcast and Magazines

## PEOPLE TO FOLLOW ON SOCIAL MEDIA

### TOP 10 ENTREPRENEURS TO FOLLOW ON FACEBOOK

Here's a list of ten entrepreneurs who have the most active pages, with the most shareable posts and videos for fellow entrepreneurs:

1. Sheryl Sandberg
   The COO of Facebook and author of *Lean In*, Sheryl is always posting the latest on women in leadership, entrepreneurship, and her own personal journey at Facebook.
2. Arnold Schwarzenegger

Arnold is a pro at Facebook, Snapchat, and Instagram. He's constantly posting on his latest adventures, and his mission to support climate action.

3. Richard Branson

   One of the world's most recognizable entrepreneurs, Richard's Facebook page is a mix of personal photos, how-to articles, and inspiring posts.

4. Randi Zuckerberg

   The older sister of Mark and founder of Zuckerberg Media, Randi is one of the most prolific users of Facebook Live video, with plenty of content for entrepreneurs and female leaders.

5. Mark Cuban

   Star of "Shark Tank" and owner of the Dallas Mavericks, Mark is always posting provocative entrepreneur-related comments and articles.

6. Mark Zuckerberg

   Mark has over 54 million followers, which isn't surprising, given that it's his social network. His posts are a mix of his personal moments at work, his baby, and his dog.

7. Marie Forleo

   Marie's page is packed with videos, interviews, and articles to support entrepreneurs, linked to her blog and Youtube channel."

8. Gary Vaynerchuk

   Gary Vee is at the forefront of what's new in social media and is the king of the hustle. You'll find plenty of live video and Q&As, as well as links to his on Youtube channel and Snapchat.

9. Mari Smith

If you're looking for the latest tips and developments to support your Facebook marketing, Mari is the go-to person. Her page is published in partnership with Facebook Business.

10. Roger James Hamilton

Posting Entrepreneur Stories from around the world.


## ENTREPRENEURS TO FOLLOW ON TWITTER

While Facebook provides great content, Twitter publishes the stream of consciousness of many of the world's top entrepreneurs in real-time. Following their tweets and using Twitter as a receiver more than a broadcaster is one of the best entrepreneur educations you can get.

Here are 25 of the most followed entrepreneurs on Twitter:

1. Oprah Winfrey
1. Bill Gates
2. Richard Branson
3. Mark Cuban
4. Lord Alan Sugar
5. Elon Musk
6. Jack Dorsey
7. Martha Stewart
8. Biz Stone
9. Tony Hsieh
10. Tony Robbins

11. Ev Williams

12. Tim O'reilly

13. Kevin Rose

14. Marissa Mayer

15. Guy Kawasaki

16. Tim Ferriss

17. Gary Vaynerchuk

18. Robert Kiyosaki

19. Steve Case

20. Roger James Hamilton

21. Robert Herjavec

22. Seth Godin

23. Kevin O'Leary

24. Daymond John

## THE DISTILLED WISDOM OF TOP ENTREPRENEURS

### *7 BILLION DOLLAR QUESTIONS*

In his book *Zero to One,* Peter Thiel puts forth the "seven questions that every market-creating business must answer."

1. The Engineering Question: Can you create breakthrough technology instead of incremental improvements?

2. The Timing Question: Is now the right time to start your particular business?

3. The Monopoly Question: Are you starting with a big share of a small market?
4. The People Question: Do you have the right team?
5. The Distribution Question: Do you have a way to not just create but deliver your product?
6. The Durability Question: Will your market position be defensible 10 and 20 years into the future?
7. The Secret Question: Have you identified a unique opportunity that others don't see?

Thiel says that if you don't have solid answers to these questions you will hit "bad luck" and fail.

## RICHARD BRANSON'S TOP 6 TIPS FOR ENTREPRENEURS

1. Listen more than you talk. Nobody learned anything by hearing themselves speak.
2. Three steps to success: Hire great talent, give them the tools to succeed, and get out of the way.
3. It is only by being bold that you get anywhere. If you are a risk-taker, then the art is to protect the downside. The brave may not live forever, but the cautious do not live at all.
4. You don't learn to walk by following rules. You learn by doing and by falling over. One thing is certain in business. You and everyone around you will make mistakes.
5. There is no greater thing you can do with your life and your

work than follow your passions in a way that serves the world and you. As soon as something stops being fun, it's time to move on. Life is too short to be unhappy.

6. If somebody offers you an amazing opportunity but you are not sure you can do it, say yes, then learn how to do it later!

## STEVE JOBS' SEVEN "RULES OF THUMB"

1. Be a yardstick of quality. Some people aren't used to an environment where excellence is expected.

2. Design is not just what it looks like and feels like. Design is how it works.

3. One of my mantras: focus and simplicity. Simple can be harder than complex.

4. Sometimes when you innovate, you make mistakes. It is best to admit them quickly, and get on with improving your other innovations."

5. The only way to do great work is to love what you do. If you haven't found it yet, keep looking.

6. For the past 33 years, I have looked in the mirror every morning and asked myself: 'If today were the last day of my life, would I want to do what I am about to do today?' And whenever the answer has been 'No' for too many days in a row, I know I need to change something.

7. Your time is limited, so don't waste it living someone else's life.

8. Overthinking leads to negative thoughts.

## THE SEVEN COMMANDMENTS
## OF ENTREPRENEURSHIP

1. Don't start a company for the money. Start a company for the mission and the money will follow.
2. Don't think small and start big. Think big and start small.
3. Don't sell to people you don't love products they don't need. Find people you love and serve them what they need.
4. Don't find a team to work for you. Find a team you want to work for.
5. Don't measure your wealth by quantity of money. Measure it by quality of time.
6. Don't set a goal to achieve a goal. Set a goal so you can be the person you need to be to achieve that goal.
7. Don't climb mountains so the world can see you. Climb mountains so you can see the world.

## THE STARTUP PARADOX

The startup paradox: to create something that scales, you need to start by doing things that don't scale. Well-known Venture Capitalist & Y Combinator co-founder, Paul Graham, wrote a famous essay called "Do Things that Don't Scale." It's one of the best essays on how to start a business.

Paul then gives nine unscalable startup tactics with examples of well-known startups who have used them to get started:

1. Recruit users manually.

   Stripe's tactic: They took user's laptops one-by-one and installed their software by hand.

2. Remember startups are fragile.

   Airbnb's tactic: They went door to door taking photos (which saved them from failing).

3. Make users very happy

   Wuloo's tactic: They sent users handwritten cards.

4. Have "insanely great" service.

   Apple's tactic: They made the packaging as great as the computers.

5. Pick a narrow market.

   Facebook's tactic: They launched only at Harvard.

6. Do things yourself.

   Pebble's tactic: They assembled the first 100 watches by hand.

7. Become their consultant.

   Viaweb's tactic: They used their own software to build stores for clients.

8. "Flintstone" under the hood.

   Stripe's tactic: They delivered 'instant' merchant accounts by signing up users by hand behind the scenes.

## MUST-READ BOOKS FOR ENTREPRENEURS

### *ON BUSINESS*

- *Tools of Titans: The Tactics, Routines, and Habits of Billionaires, Icons, and World-Class Performers* by Tim Ferriss

- *The Lean Startup: How Today's Entrepreneurs Use Continuous Innovation to Create Radically Successful Businesses* by Eric Ries
- *Foundr V1.0: Lessons From The Greatest Entrepreneurs Today* by Nathan Chan
- *The War of Art* by Steven Pressfield
- *How to Win Friends and Influence People* by Dale Carnegie
- *The 4-Hour Workweek: Escape 9-5, Live Anywhere, and Join the New Rich* by Tim Ferriss
- *Influence: The Psychology of Persuasion* by Robert B Cialdini
- *Unshakeable: Your Financial Freedom Playbook* by Tony Robbins
- *Start with Why: How Great Leaders Inspire Everyone to Take Action* by Simon Sinek

## ON LIFE

- *Think and Grow Rich* by Napoleon Hill
- *Awaken the Giant Within: How to Take Immediate Control of Your Mental, Emotional, Physical and Financial* by Tony Robbins
- *Man's Search for Meaning* by Viktor E. Frankl and Harold S. Kushner
- *Mindset: The New Psychology of Success* by Carol Dweck
- *Principles: Life and Work* by Ray Dalio
- *The Alchemist* by Paulo Coelho
- *The Subtle Art of Not Giving a F\*ck: A Counterintuitive Approach to Living a Good Life* by Mark Manson
- *The Start-up of You: Adapt to the Future, Invest in Yourself, and Transform Your Career* by Reid Hoffman

- *The Four Agreements: A Practical Guide to Personal Freedom* by Don Miguel Ruiz
- *The Untethered Soul: The Journey Beyond Yourself* by Michael A. Singer

For more book recommendations on learning, please refer to "Learn Anything Faster" chapter.


## PODCASTS + MAGAZINES

### PODCASTS

- How I Built This
- The Ultimate Entrepreneur
- Tim Ferriss Show
- School of Greatness
- The GaryVee Audio Experience
- The Tony Robbins Podcast
- The Top Entrepreneurs in Money, Marketing, Business and Life
- I Love Marketing
- Tai Lopez "Book of the Day"


### MAGAZINES

- *Foundr Magazine*
- *Business Insider*
- *Inc.*

- *Forbes*
- *Fortune*
- *Entrepreneur*

**PART 3**

# WHAT TO DO

## CHAPTER 25

# SET BOLD GOALS

---

*"If your dreams don't scare you, they are too small."*

— RICHARD BRANSON

*"There is no passion to be found playing small — in settling for a life that is less than the one you are capable of living."*

— NELSON MANDELA

When it comes to achieving anything, the first step is setting a goal. It's a fundamental key to all lifelong success plans. The concept of goal-setting isn't exactly ground-breaking, but here's the reality: most people don't have a clearly defined set of goals. And more than that, the goal-setting process that we are talking about goes far beyond merely speaking in the affirmative and having a vision for something greater.

Furthermore, we are not only talking about goals. We are talking about big goals. Why? Because, while we may not achieve our big goals, **if we do not even attempt to think big, then we are definitely not going to achieve our big goals.** In addition, most things in life seem harder to achieve than they actually are.

## WHY WE NEED GOALS?

When, 20 years later in 1973, researchers went back and interviewed the surviving class members of the class of 1953 . . . to find out what their lives were like. They noted that the 3% that had written their goals for a specific plan seemed to be happier and more well-adjusted than the others. Of course, that is subjective. But they also found that the 3% group was worth more in financial terms than the other 97% who did not have clear goals. This is the power of goals. Goals allow us to create our future in advance. They allow us to envision our destiny, and, in turn, shape our lives. They give us direction and hope.[1]

The following are four tips around goal setting from peak performance strategist Tony Robbins.

### WRITE IT DOWN

Write your goals down — not on a computer, but on paper

or in a journal. Research has shown that there's something special that happens when we write something down. You become a creator when you write down your goals. You are acknowledging to both your conscious and subconscious that where you are right now is not where you want to be. Your brain then makes this distinction and becomes dissatisfied.

**One of the strongest motivators is a sense of dissatisfaction.** When you're totally comfortable and relaxed, you're not going to be motivated to do whatever it takes to make things happen. Dissatisfaction is a power that you want. Use this as a tool to influence yourself so you can start to take actionable steps toward your success.

## GET CLEAR ON THE "WHY"

Get crystal clear. Write out the details — how would achieving this goal make you feel? What would that mean to you? How will it change your life?

By getting absolutely clear as to why you must achieve your goal, you will find your purpose. The purpose of a goal is stronger than the outcome, because the purpose of a goal is not so you can get the result. The purpose of a goal is what the end result will make you as a person.

Knowing this purpose will help keep you laser-focused, and

it will help get you through the rough times. If you create a strong enough "why" to keep you going, you will have the fuel to endure anything that comes your way. Ultimately, material objects or a certain title will not make you happy. The only thing that will make you happy is the person you have become and what you have created in your lifetime.

So ask yourself: what are the reasons that you must achieve your goal? How will it change your life for the better? What lies underneath? How will achieving that goal make you feel?

## FIND ABSOLUTE CERTAINTY

It's perfectly okay to have no idea how you are going to achieve your goal. And it's perfectly okay to set goals that go beyond your present ability or skill. What's important here is that you operate from absolute total belief and faith.

Frame your goals with absolute certainty — that no matter what, you will find a way to make it happen. Even if it seems impossible to you now, you know in your core that you can pull it off. When you have that fundamental belief, you will be taking back control of your life. Regardless of the fact that you may not be able to control the outside world or the challenges that come your way, know that you will persevere and overcome.

Too many people give up prematurely because they focus on the outcome and then stop and tell themselves, "I don't know how to do that," or "I could never achieve that." But what if you didn't have to figure out how to do it, but rather, believe that you will figure it out no matter what? That achieving your goal is not only within the realm of possibilities, it is an absolute certainty? Just imagine how that could change your life right now. Capture that certainty.

## PRACTICE AND REPEAT

Think about the greatest coaches of all-time: Vince Lombardi and John Wooden, for example. They were famous for teaching the fundamentals to individuals who were already the best at what they did. And they did it over and over again. Why? Because repetition is the mother of skill.

You cannot set goals one time, never look at them again — and then expect long-term results. Your subconscious mind may know the general direction to move in, but the power comes from daily practice and constant review. **People looking for a quick fix will never achieve mastery.** Reaching your goals takes focus and practice: You have to repeat it over and over again.[2]

Last but not least, make sure to schedule the actions you will take on your calendar so you can start the process of turning the goal into reality.

## ACTION CHECKLIST

☐ Write down the 3 most important goals you want to achieve in the next 12 months.

☐ Write down the 3 reasons why you must achieve those goals.

☐ Find absolute certainty by committing to the goal, reading stories of people who have achieved the goal, or whatever it takes.

☐ Create a monthly goal and plan based on the 12-month goals.

☐ Schedule milestones on your calendar.

☐ Revisit the Time Management chapter to schedule your goals!

## CHAPTER 26

# SET UP YOUR DAY TO WIN

———

*"When you arise in the morning, think of what a precious privilege it is to be alive — to breathe, to think, to enjoy, to love."*

— MARCUS AURELIUS

*"Routine, in an intelligent man, is a sign of ambition."*

— W. H. AUDEN

Morning sets the tone for the day, period. If you win the morning, you win the day. Many successful people have morning rituals or routines they use to help them win the day. After a great morning ritual, you feel excited, focused, calm, confident, and ready to take on the day. Imagine what a difference it would make if you felt like this every morning.

In short, this chapter will show you an effective way to hack your day, which is to hack your morning. To be more precise, you need to hack the first 60-90 mins of your day. Pay attention to things you do in the morning and how they make you feel. And from there, we hack and optimize it. The following are some of the powerful morning rituals and frameworks from some of the most successful entrepreneurs I know.

## FIVE MORNING RITUALS TO HELP WIN THE DAY[1]

If you listen to Tim Ferriss' podcast, which I strongly recommend, one of the first questions he always asks is, "What does the first 60-90mins of your day look like?" After asking 100+ world-class performers about their morning rituals, Tim tested different practices and found these five things that worked best for him.

1. Make Your Bed (< 2mins)

   It gives you a sense of accomplishment by finishing the first task in the day. In addition, this practice provides a sense of control you have over your life, while most things in your life are out of your control.

2. Meditate (10-20 mins)

   Again, almost 80% of all people Tim interviews do some form of meditation on a daily basis. Check out chapter X for details on meditation.

3. Do 5-10 Reps of Something to wake up the body (<1 min)

This is not working out. Rather, you want to wake up and "prime" your state of mind and body. Getting into the body, even for 30 seconds, Tim notices a drastic change in his mood and quieting of his mental chatter. You can do push-ups, squats, sit ups, pull ups, and or any stretching routine. (In the following section, I describe Tony Robbins' Priming Exercise.)

4. Prepare "Titanium Tea" (2-3 mins)

   Tim noted this combo is great for cognition and fat loss. If you are interested in the recipe, search his website.

5. Five-Minute Journal (5-10 mins)

   Write down three things you are grateful for, three things that would make today great, and three positive daily affirmations that start with "I am."


## TONY ROBBINS ON PRIMING[2]

Priming is one of the most powerful practices I have experienced. It was designed to prime the nervous system to focus on the constructive emotions and thoughts. It's a powerful ritual that involves powerful and directed breathing and movement to center yourself so that you're primed for whatever the day brings. It might feel strange at first—but if you practice priming regularly, you'll experience an incredible shift in the quality of your thoughts and emotions.

Priming only takes ten minutes. And, as Tony says, "If you don't have ten minutes, you don't have a life."

1. Perform a breathing exercise.

   Begin by sitting straight with your eyes closed. Inhale deeply through your nostrils while simultaneously lifting your arms in a shoulder press motion, and then exhale forcefully through your nostrils while bringing your arms back to your body, palms up. Perform the breaths in quick succession.

2. Express gratitude.

3. Take a few minutes to think of three things you are grateful for, spending about a minute on each.

4. Experience connection.

5. Imagine a light flowing into the top of your head and then spreading into the rest of your body, strengthening and healing you. When it has flowed through your entire body, then visualize that energy flowing out from your body to the world around you. You can focus on loved ones, as well as total strangers who may be in your vicinity.

6. Visualize success.

7. Spend the last three minutes visualizing what it is like to achieve three goals. Don't think about making it happen; rather, see it as done. Spend a minute on each.

## THE MIRACLE MORNING: THE NOT-SO-OBVIOUS SECRET GUARANTEED TO TRANSFORM YOUR LIFE (BEFORE 8 A.M.)[3]

After being hit by a car and declared dead for six minutes, spending six days in a coma and being told he would never walk again, today Hal Elrod is a top keynote speaker, bestselling author, entrepreneur, and ultra-marathoner. He attributes his change mainly to the six-step Miracle Morning System as summarized below. Hal even created a very simple acronym to memorize the habits. He calls them his Life S.A.V.E.R.S.

First and foremost, wake up before 7 a.m. The reason is simple; the morning is the time that you are most likely not have interruptions. People won't be demanding your attention via emails, messages, and more. Do you want to know the key to wake up early that I discovered after countless failed attempts? The key is to go sleep early, which takes more discipline that you expect. But this is the only sustainable way to way up early. Most people do not spend the last couple hours of the day in a productive way anyways.

- S: *Silence* — Sit in silence or meditation even for as little one minute.
- A: *Affirmations* — Use affirmations to get yourself in a positive state.
- V: *Visualize* — Visualize the outcomes you want to create.
- E: *Exercise* — Work out, if only for just five minutes.
- R: *Read* — Choose something that either educates or inspires you. I found this practice very effective to remind myself to raise my standards.
- S: *Scribe* — Write in a journal, following any method for at least 15 minutes.

## ACTION CHECKLIST

☐ Create your own morning ritual with 5 things you want to do.

☐ Practice your morning ritual for 2 weeks.

☐ Try different practices to find out the ones that make you feel the best and adjust accordingly.

☐ Schedule it! Be sure to wake up and practice your rituals before you start your day. This will take planning.

## CHAPTER 27

# CREATE A STRONG PEER GROUP

———

*"You are the average of five people you spend the most time with."*

—JIM ROHN

*"Set your life on fire. Seek those who fan your flames."*

— RUMI

"Tony, are people just lazy in nature? I don't know why our soldiers all drop their standards after the leave the military. They stop working out and improving themselves. They simply drop their commitment to be their best. They were all the best of the best." Tony Robbins was doing a seminar for the USMC, and the special force commander asked this question

"No sir," Tony responded. "They drop their standards because people's lives are a direct reflection of the expectation of his/her peer group."

Have you heard the saying, "You are who your friends are"? You might have heard it from your parents in grade school, when groups started to form around different personalities and interests. Cliques start to form, often centered around similar expectations and behaviors—watching the same television shows and movies, forming similar habits, and even speaking and dressing like each other. Even though cliques are probably most prevalent in high school, the power of groups should not be overlooked in college.

This all seems fairly innocuous at first, but ultimately, you become who you hang around with, or "the company you keep." And after college, the same principle applies. The difference is we are more conscious of the influence our peers have on us; we know better than to fall in with the wrong crowd. Yet, we need to be more vigilant about our surroundings and choosing a group of people that will elevate us, not bring us down.

Who are your peers? People who you care enough about that you are willing to change your behavior to get their acceptance.

## THIS IS ONE OF THE MOST IMPORTANT AND POWERFUL HACKS IN THIS BOOK

Changing who you spend time with is probably the most effective way of changing your behaviors. When people are together, their expectations and standards influence each other naturally. There is a lot of intention or resistance to change, but this influence just happens naturally. For example, have you ever stopped make a major positive change in your life because that's not how your peers normally behave? It might look "weird" to do some things that you know you should do? If yes, then the influence described above is working against you in a subtle but powerful way.

## DO YOU LOOK UP TO THE PEOPLE YOU SURROUND YOURSELF WITH?

This doesn't mean that they have to be multi-millionaires when you're just trying to focus on getting a better job. Looking up to those around you can be as easy as admiring the way they speak, the way they carry themselves, their accomplishments, the way they solve problems, or their general approach to daily life. Respect is a powerful motivator.

## DO YOUR PEERS EMBODY QUALITIES THAT YOU WANT?

Sometimes we meet people that blow us away. Do you know

someone with so much charisma and positivity that you are intrigued by their very nature, and maybe even crave their company? Or perhaps someone with a collection of positive habits and demonstrated discipline that you think, "I wish I had that. How do they do that?" Whatever qualities you want to acquire, surround yourself with people who have them.

## LOOK AT THE FIVE PEOPLE YOU SPEND THE MOST TIME WITH

If you take a good hard look at the people you hang around with the most, then do some self-reflecting on who you are, you will find that you are the average sum of them all—almost as if you carry a little piece of each of them with you. Do you want all of those pieces? If not, it could be time to re-evaluate your decisions.[1]

Changing peer group is a hard change to make, especially if people who you spend most time with are not the kind of people you aspire to be or if your family does not include strong role models. Tony advises, "Love your family, but choose your peers." You can still love and care about your family and old friends. On the other hand, choose to spend more time with people who have qualities that you want and let them influence you instead.

## ACTION CHECKLIST

☐ Audit the 5 people you spend the most time with.

☐ Identify qualities that you want most.

☐ Identify people who have those qualities.

☐ Reach out to them and start to spend time with them.

## CHAPTER 28

# BUILD ON YOUR STRENGTHS

---

*"Hide not your talents. They for use were made. What's a sundial in the shade?"*

— BENJAMIN FRANKLIN

*"The superheroes you have in your mind (idols, icons, titans, billionaires, etc.) are nearly all walking flaws who've maximized 1 or 2 strengths."*

— TIM FERRISS

Many top entrepreneurs believe that trying to improve on weaknesses is one of the biggest lies and time wasters. Instead, they think the better way is to double down on your strengths. I found this way of thinking novel when I first heard it.

**Never focus on a weakness because you can't be great at something you are not good at.** Schools taught us the opposite. Most students focus on improving what they bad at instead of pursuing their strengths. In the real world, it becomes people trying to fix their weakness instead of focusing on developing their strengths.

Strength has two meanings. First, things you are good at. Second, how you best function as a person. The first kind is more obvious. You are good at math and not good at writing. The second kind is more subtle. For example, if you are good at logic but bad at memorization, focusing on your strength would mean to study by adding in as much logic to the materials you need to remember as possible. We all have different strengths and weakness, and now is the best time in your life to identify and optimize your strengths. If you are a big picture person, handing details would be difficult and time-consuming for you. However, for a person who is more detail oriented, he or she will have a much easier and pleasant time handling the task. In the case of writing this book, knowing I'm not good at grammar and editing, I can't express the sense of relief and comfort I felt knowing that my editor has my back.

Roger Hamilton, the creator of one of the best personality/ strength tests called Wealth Dynamics, explained the difference between working hard or hard work.[1]

**The Right Way:** Working hard is about doubling down on what you're best at and love most. When you work hard in your genius and in your flow, it doesn't feel like hard work. The reward is in the work, because you keep getting better at what you're best at.

**The Wrong Way:** Hard work is the opposite of working hard. It's when you work on the things you're not greatest at. It's when you feel like you're swimming upstream, and life becomes a struggle. Instead of every hour leaving you more energized, it leaves you more exhausted.

We all have the same 24 hours of time. Use yours wisely. Are you in your flow? Or out of the flow? What do you need to change, and who do you need to surround yourself with so their strengths match your weaknesses, and everyone can work hard at what they're best at?

Doubling down on your strength also means you need to know your weaknesses, which most people fail to do. Most people avoid facing their weaknesses, so that their weakness becomes a key chokehold. For example, if an entrepreneur is bad at management and never addresses it, this bad management would prevent the company from growing to the next stage. On the other hand, if the entrepreneur has the courage to face his weaknesses, he could enroll a team member who is good at management to make up for his weakness.

Ray Dalio, an iconic investor and entrepreneur, put enormous focus on the importance of the ability to access oneself and others objectively. Ray elegantly explained objective assessment and how to handle weaknesses in his new book *Principles: Life and Work*, which I highly recommend to everyone reading this book. The rest of this chapter is an excerpt from Ray's new book.

"Successful people are those who can go above themselves to see things objectively and manage those things to shape change. They can take in the perspectives of others instead of being trapped in their own heads with their own biases. **They are able to look objectively at what they are like— their strengths and weaknesses—and what others are like to put the right people in the right roles to achieve their goals. Once you understand how to do this you'll see that there's virtually nothing you can't accomplish.**

You will just have to learn how to face your realities and use the full range of resources at your disposal. For example, if you as the designer/manager discover that you as the worker can't do something well, you need to fire yourself as the worker and get a good replacement, while staying in the role of designer/ manager of your own life. You shouldn't be upset if you find out that you're bad at something—you should be happy that you found out, because knowing that and dealing with it will improve your chances of getting what you want.

If you are disappointed because you can't be the best person to do everything yourself, you are terribly naive. **Nobody can do everything well. Would you want to have Einstein on your basketball team?** When he fails to dribble and shoot well, would you think badly of him? Should he feel humiliated? **Imagine all the areas in which Einstein was incompetent, and imagine how hard he struggled to excel even in the areas in which he was the best in the world**. Watching people struggle and having others watch you struggle can elicit all kinds of ego-driven emotions such as sympathy, pity, embarrassment, anger, or defensiveness. **You need to get over all that and stop seeing struggling as something negative. Most of life's greatest opportunities come out of moments of struggle; it's up to you to make the most of these tests of creativity and character.**

When encountering your weaknesses you have four choices:

1. You can deny them (which is what most people do).
2. You can accept them and work at them in order to try to convert them into strengths (which might or might not work depending on your ability to change).
3. You can accept your weaknesses and find ways around them.
4. Or, you can change what you are going after. Which solution you choose will be critically important to the direction of your life.

The worst path you can take is the first. Denial can only lead to your constantly banging up against your weaknesses, having pain, and not getting anywhere. The second—accepting your weaknesses while trying to turn them into strengths—is probably the best path if it works. But some things you will never be good at and it takes a lot of time and effort to change. The best single clue as to whether you should go down this path is whether the thing you are trying to do is consistent with your nature (i.e., your natural abilities). The third path—accepting your weaknesses while trying to find ways around them—is the easiest and typically the most viable path, yet it is the one least followed. The fourth path, changing what you are going after, is also a great path, though it requires flexibility on your part to get past your preconceptions and enjoy the good fit when you find it."[2]

## ACTION CHECKLIST

- ☐ Identify your top 5 strengths in terms of what you are good at and how do you function the best.
- ☐ Identify your top 5 weakness using the same framework.
- ☐ Check out Wealth Dynamics.
- ☐ Focus on developing your strength and using your strength to help you.

## CHAPTER 29

# GET STRONGER, LITERALLY

—

*"Doing anything well requires energy, and you just have a lot more energy when you're fit. I make sure I work out at least three times a week—usually first thing when I wake up."*

— MARK ZUCKERBERG

*"Do not wish it was easier, wish you were better."*

— JIM ROHN

"I seriously doubt that I would have been as successful in my career (and happy in my personal life) if I hadn't always placed importance on my health and fitness," Richard Branson said. "I definitely can achieve twice as much by keeping fit," Branson explained to a reporter. "It keeps the brain functioning well."[1]

When Richard Branson was asked how he battles stress, he thought for a while and then said, "I work out."

When volunteering at a Tony Robbins event, I was excited to see Enhamed Enhamed, a blind Olympic champion swimmer, was also part of the crew. I really wanted to talk to him and learn from him. When I first saw him at another one of Tony's events, I thought he was a blind person who overcame many difficulties in life, including suicide attempts at a young age, and who is now living a fulfilling and inspiring life, and that was impressive enough. However, what I learned is that Enhamed has set four World Records in his career as a swimmer and won four Gold Medals at the Paralympics in Beijing 2008, and many other medals.

"Wow," I thought and promptly had a battle with my fear of rejection for an hour. Finally, I decided to go up to Enhamed and just chat. He was extremely friendly and welcoming, which showed me again that our mind is very good at creating fear and unnecessary stress to stop us from doing things. After introducing myself and getting to know Enhamed a little better, I started to eagerly ask my questions: What is your best piece of advice for students? "Work out every day, even just for 20 minutes. Did you know it improves brain function as well? If you do not even have 20 minutes, you know it is an excuse."

I proceeded with another question. "You have been through

many difficulties that most people cannot even imagine, and today you are happy, motivated, and inspiring many others. What would you say to people who just complain about little things all the time?" Enhamed gave me an answer that I will never forget in my life. **"Do not wish life to get easier, wish you were stronger."**

What an insight! We always talk about be strong, but most people never take it literally. I mean, it makes sense to first be literally physically strong, right? As a person who has not been successful at keeping a regular workout routine, I told myself, "If you cannot get strong physically and literally, forget about being strong and successful mentally or metaphorically." Well, that was a good wakeup call.

We all know it is good to work out and exercise. I don't need to include more studies and stats here. But what does it have to do with entrepreneurship?

- It is a good measurement for prioritization and time management. If you know it's very important, but you "don't have time" to do it, there is something to improve.
- It teaches you to push through resistance and start. At the beginning, most people do not like to work out. So it is a great tool to train your brain to push through and do the right thing.
- It develops your persistence through challenges.
- It helps you to maintain a strong mind and emotional state by

producing endorphins that make you feel happy, strong, certain, and free after a good workout.

Seth Goldman, co-founder of Honest Tea, one of the entrepreneurs I interviewed for this book, believes that **running is the perfect sport for entrepreneurs.** He actually published a blog post laying out arguments for his position. Let's look at Seth's six reasons below.

## 1. IT'S CHEAP AND EASY

Every bootstrap entrepreneur can appreciate something that's cost effective and doesn't make us dependent on someone else's schedule. If you own a pair of running shoes, you can be a runner.

## 2. IT'S ENERGIZING

Cash may be the fire that keeps an enterprise alive, but the entrepreneur's personal energy is the oxygen. Without a sense of enthusiasm and passion, the founder will fail to inspire confidence in employees, investors, vendors, customers, not to mention the worried partner or family. So we need to find ways to continually refuel. Contrary to the perception that exercise saps a person's energy, I find daily exertion increases my energy level.

### 3. IT RELIEVES STRESS

Entrepreneurs face pressure from all directions, and the tension can be overwhelming. Running doesn't make problems disappear, but it can create rare, solitary moments to gain perspective. And, just as important, running creates moments when I can't take immediate action to deal with the challenges I'm facing. (I never run with a phone!)

### 4. IT PROVIDES MOMENTS IN NATURE

Too much of life is spent in windowless, air-conditioned rooms that are disconnected from the natural world. In addition to getting fresh air, spending an hour in nature also helps instill a sense of humility. When things are going well, it's not hard for an entrepreneur to gain an inflated sense of power. But an hour outside helps remind us that we have much less control over the world than we imagine.

### 5. IT TEACHES ENDURANCE AND PERSEVERANCE

In addition to the obvious reminder that scaling an enterprise is a marathon, not a sprint, distance training helps develop the physical stamina required to handle the long hours and the travel demands that are standards in the life of an entrepreneur. It also helps reinforce that there is no shortcut to success.

## 6. IT GETS YOUR COMPETITIVE JUICES FLOWING

Every entrepreneur has a competitive streak, and, while in business we may need to diplomatically suppress our desire to crush our opponents, it's fun to occasionally be blatantly competitive. Though it can be fun to compete in my age group at a road race, it can also be energizing to run against myself—an occasional run with a GPS watch, or on a track, helps me gauge my pace and fitness level.[2]

## ACTION CHECKLIST

- ☐ Start to work out every morning for at least 10 mins for a week. Pay attention to how you feel afterwards.
- ☐ Do resistance training 2-3 times a week for a month. See how you feel.
- ☐ Take 5-10 min breaks when you are working or studying for long hours. Move your body versus just switching to another website. Go outside, walk, jog, or do some simple exercises (push up, squads, etc) inside. Notice how it makes you feel.
- ☐ If you're very out of shape, find a website like "The Couch to 5k in 9 weeks running program" to guide you.
- ☐ Find someone one campus to work out with. There may be aspiring physical trainers who will work with you, or a group of students who hold each other accountable for working out. Remember to raise your peer group in this area of your life too!

## CHAPTER 30

# BE THE HUMBLEST PERSON YOU KNOW

———

*"I believe the first test of a truly great man is in his humility."*

— JOHN RUSKIN

Why should we be humble? Because is there always more to learn. You probably already know that my favorite kind of learning is to model people who already accomplished what you want to achieve. Nathan Chan, the founder of *Foundr Magazine*, shares the same attitude. Since its start in 2013, *Foundr Magazine* has interviewed many of the most iconic entrepreneurs in the world and gained more than 250,000 subscribers. Nathan attributes a big part of his success to learning from other really smart founders and people who inspire him. To put it simply, Nathan said, "I just flat out learn from them." At the same time, he points out that it's easier said than done because it takes networking, building relationships, and providing value to the other person first.

We are not talking about the being shy and avoiding eye contact kind of humility. That is outward humility that many people in the world have. But there is a big difference between being outwardly humble versus inwardly humble.

When you think of Michael Jordan, he might appear to be one of the most confident and even cockiest guy you know. He is not at all outwardly humble. However, his coaches have a different perspective. In the book *Michael Jordan: The Life* one of his coaches remarks, "I've never seen a player listen so closely to what the coach said and go do it." So, if you wonder about the secrets that made Jordan into arguably the best basketball player in history, his coach just told you. First, the ability to listen. Second, go do it.

However, most people respond in a way that is the opposite of what Jordan does. They are outwardly humble, but inwardly cocky. You don't believe this? Ok, you can test out your level of humility by answering the following questions. Rate yourself on a scale of 0-10, average them out, and get your "Net Humility Score."[1]

1.   How many mentors have you tracked down to help you with whatever goal you're trying to accomplish?

2. How many times have you asked for help from experts?

3. How many nonfiction books have you read in the past year?

4. How many interviews or podcasts have you listened to on the areas you want to improve?

5. How many seminars or conferences have you attended in the past year?

If you are like most people, you probably have some very low numbers. And it will continue to be this way until you decide to set a different standard for your level of humility, in comparison to the rest of the world.

Now let's look at an epitome of humility from one of the greatest entrepreneurs of all time—Sam Watson. There's a great story about how humility landed Sam Watson in a Brazilian Jail. There was once a group of Brazilian businessmen who sent letters to the heads of the top ten U.S. retailers asking to come visit and learn how they did business. Most of the U.S. companies ignored the letters, and the few that acknowledged the Brazilians said, "No." However, Sam Walton said, "Yes."

Sam Walton invited them to his hometown in Bentonville, Arkansas, and, when the Brazilian businessmen came, Sam ended up answering their questions with far more questions because he wanted to see what he could learn from them.

The story gets even better. Sam Walton later went to Brazil to visit the businessmen and ended up getting arrested in the process. The cops thought he was suspicious because they found him on his hands and knees measuring the amount of space between the aisles at a grocery store. They thought he was nuts, so they locked him up. In fact, he was just always studying the competition and was always "on," and willing to dig in and get dirty.

Even though he was one of the richest men in the United States, Sam Walton was humble enough to get on his hands and knees measuring things because he understood that there was always more he could learn.

Even the smartest people in the world recognize that this world is simply too vast for them to have a complete understanding of it. There's a reason both Bill Gates and Warren Buffett both said that if they could choose any superpower, they'd choose the ability to read faster than anyone else in the world. They see that there's still so much they have to learn, and if that's the case for them, it definitely holds true for me and you as well.

I am not going to repeat why it's important for you to read more books and watch more interviews and things like that. That should be a given by this point. **I want to encourage you to raise the bar and start to go to conferences and seminars.** First, because immersion is the best way to learn. Second, you will make great connections with people who are also humble, driven, and share in similar interests. Third, you might meet your future mentors. The psychological distance at conferences and seminars is one of the shortest, because you are attending alongside the people who are much more successful than you; you are all in the audience together.

I have spent more than 1,500 hours at seminars and conferences. In addition to the incredible content I have learned, I made some of my best friends, mentors, and connections there. I have skipped classes and exams to go to seminars, because I know which one gives me more value and growth for the time spent.

Embark on this journey of being humble AND hungry, you might discover a different "you," if not a different world.

## ACTION CHECKLIST

- ☐ Create a plan for how to improve your humility score.
- ☐ Identify 3 subjects that you want to learn the most.
- ☐ Identify 5 people who might be potential mentors. Reach out to them.
- ☐ Double check you are taking the actions suggested in the "A-Book-A-Day" and "Listen" chapters.
- ☐ Look at Tony Robbins. Check out his content. Watch the

documentary called "I Am Not Your Guru." Go attend "Unleash the Power Within" (UPW) seminar if you have the opportunity.

☐ Look for other mentors and conferences that interest you and organize yourself to include these in your "education."

# CHAPTER 31

# LISTEN

———

*"Listen more than you talk. Nobody learned anything by hearing themselves speak."*

— RICHARD BRANSON

*"I like to listen. I have learned a great deal from listening carefully. Most people never listen."*

— ERNEST HEMINGWAY

Do you want to be considered a great communicator or conversationalist after a conversation? Here is a quick and easy hack: let the other person do 90% of the talking. Even better, guide the conversation with thoughtful questions.

Richard Branson supports this hack. "It is a strange facet of the human condition, but, invariably, when you engage in a

30-minute dialogue with someone and manage the conversation in such a way that you get the other person to talk for 25 of the 30 minutes, the person who you allowed to do all the talking is highly likely to go away impressed by what a great conversationalist you are."[1]

A famous entrepreneur and marketing guru Jay Abraham has had similar experiences. After a conversation in which he asked several questions because he was simply curious about the other person, Jay was surprised to hear, "You are one of the most interesting people I've ever met." Jay was very surprised at first, but after many similar incidences, he now recommends his practice of active listening.

I think it's safe to assume that everyone likes to talk about themselves. If, on the other hand, you yourself have spoken for 25 of the 30 minutes, the other will party most likely be thinking, "What a talker! I couldn't even open my mouth."

*The Virgin Way: If It's Not Fun, It's Not Worth Doing* is a book Richard Branson wrote to collect everything he knows about leadership. The first chapter of this leadership book is about listening. It is easy to see the emphasis this iconic entrepreneur puts on listening. Below are some tips on effective listening from Richard's book.[2]

1. **Listening while keeping your mouth shut** and saying nothing is much smarter than not listening, speaking up, and saying nothing. Instead of really listening, many of people focus on frequently interjecting their comments and questions, and they think, mistakenly, that this makes them look smart.

2. **Don't focus on what you are going to say.** Most people operate on the flawed assumption that they know what the speaker is going to say. Instead of listening, their focus shifts entirely to trying to formulate "smart" questions. In addition to the sheer rudeness of their constant interruptions, such people usually only succeed in looking foolish.

3. **It all comes back to note-taking.** Rather than constantly interrupting a speaker with self-serving questions, it is smarter (and more polite) to note down comments and questions, and save them for later in the conversation.

4. A really skilled listener not only takes in what has been said, but will also **hear what has not been said.** One of the easiest examples of this leads to questions such as, "I was intrigued to note that you failed to make any mention of XYZ. Does this mean you don't consider it relevant to your proposal?"

5. Similarly, **pay close attention to the way that they say what they say, to "read between the lines."** The real story is often dramatically different from what the casual listener might understand is being said "on the lines."[3]

## THE POWER OF GOOD QUESTIONS

The hack of asking thoughtful questions will get you amazing answers, as well as stories to listen to and learn from. It's the best tool to use when you want to learn from someone, especially when that person is a lot more experienced and successful than you are. As a bonus, thoughtful questions will also help make you appear smart and respectful of the other person's time, which leads to a better impression. Also, using follow-up questions is a great way to dig deeper on certain topics and make the flow of the conversation more natural.

When I want to learn from someone, I ask a lot of the same questions. Here are my favorites:

1. Why did you decide to pursue your career?
2. What have been the best moments in your life/career?
3. What are the three most important things you have learned (in your career or life)?
4. What books would you recommend on X?
5. What books do you give to people most often?
6. What would you tell you 20-year old self?
7. What is the best advice you have received?
8. How do you define success?
9. If you could teach one course in college on anything, what would you teach and why?
10. What are the factors that contributed the most to your success? Why?

11. What are the most helpful beliefs you have? Why?

12. What are the most helpful/beneficial habits or routines you have?

13. What separates people who are good from those that are great at X.

14. What were the most important decisions you've made?

15. What are your goals? (See if I can be of any help, and offer it!)

16. If you could only give one piece of advice on life, what would it be?

17. What do you value the most?

18. Who do you look up to?

## ACTION CHECKLIST

☐ Listen to people will all your attention and appropriate eye contact. (Turn off your phone!)

☐ Start to apply Richard Branson's suggestions.

☐ Start to interview people you look up to with effective listening hacks and your favorite questions from the list.

## CHAPTER 32

# FOLLOW WARREN BUFFETT'S A-BOOK-A-DAY DIET

———

*"If we encounter a man of rare intellect, we should ask him what books he reads."*

— RALPH WALDO EMERSON

*"The book you don't read won't help."*

— JIM ROHN

*"The person you will be in five years depends largely on the information you feed your mind today. Be picky about the books*

*you read, the people you spend time with, and the conversation
you engage in."*

— RUBEN CHAVEZ

The purpose of reading is to help you learn whatever you
want to learn and maybe offer some inspiration. For sure, it
is not the only way, but it is for sure the most accessible and
cost-effective way.

One way of looking at reading fascinated me: a fast and cheap
way to learn something that someone spent decades on trying
to figure it out; it's kind of like cheating. Reading seemed
more appealing to me after I started to think of reading this
way. Someone once said, stop complaining about how it is
hard to get a great mentor; great books are your mentors. It
is true. How likely is it for Bill Gates, Richard Branson, Mark
Zuckerberg to be your mentor? Those people are busy, like
really busy. But you can read books by them and learn amazing lessons.

If we really keep the outcome of learning valuable lessons
in mind, we can read a lot faster. **Remember, no one said
you have to read a book cover to cover. If this belief is still
limiting you from reading, STOP IT.** Replace reading with
a better metaphor: gold mining. You are just looking for the
gold, so stop feeling bad about not examining every piece of
rock. You are not in middle school anymore.

Books are here to serve you by giving you the specific knowledge or information you are looking for. The following is a guideline for reading a book a day in 30-60 minutes.

- Spend 3 minutes skim through the table of contents and the structure of the book.
- Write down 3-5 questions you want to get answered by the book (you are helping your brain a lot by giving it targets)
- Skim through the book to find the answers (and learn to get comfortable about skipping irrelevant pages).

I read mostly non-fiction books and self-development books, and my personal takeaways are not generally from the specific techniques or information I learned. Instead, I gain inspiration, energy, and inspiration from the authors or stories of people who are living life fully. I find it sometimes to be a gateway to allow myself to look at my life from a higher perspective instead of being busy with all the daily tasks cluttering up my life.

The emergence and popularity of audiobooks officially killed the excuse that "I do not have time to read." Did you know a normal book is only five or six hours in length? That means, if you listen to a book for an hour in a day with NET time (No Extra Time)—when you are eating breakfast, commuting to work, working out, or a similar activity—you will be able to finish a book a week. That's 52 books a year. I find Audible from Amazon to be the best audiobook site/app because of the number of books and the option to switch back and forth between the audio version and the Kindle version.

What is the one habit ultra-successful people have in common? They read. A lot.

In fact, when Warren Buffett was once asked about the key to success, he pointed to a stack of nearby books and said, "Read 500 pages like this every day. That's how knowledge works. It builds up, like compound interest. All of you can do it, but I guarantee not many of you will do it."[1]

- Warren Buffett takes this habit to the extreme. He read between 600 and 1000 pages per day when he was beginning his investing career, and he still devotes about 80% of each day to reading.
- Bill Gates reads about 50 books per year, which breaks down to about one per week.
- Mark Cuban reads more than three hours every day.
- Elon Musk is an avid reader. When he was asked how he taught himself "rocket science'" he thought for a while and said quietly "I read books. Many books."
- Mark Zuckerberg resolved to read a book every two weeks throughout 2015.
- Oprah Winfrey selects one of her favorite books every month for her Book Club members to read and discuss. Oprah described

reading as a comfortable place she can escape to in the midst of the business of this world.

And these aren't just isolated examples. A study of 1,200 wealthy people found that they all have reading as a pastime in common.[2] But successful people don't just read anything. They are highly selective about what they read, opting to be educated over being entertained. They believe that books are a gateway to learning, knowledge, and inspiration. In particular, they obsess over biographies and autobiographies of other successful people for guidance and inspiration.

There are many examples of successful people dropping out of school or foregoing a formal education, but it is clear that they never stop learning. **Reading is a key part of their success.**

## ACTION CHECKLIST

- ☐ Find at least 5 books on a topic that interests you the most.
- ☐ Get the majority of the books you pick in Kindle and audio so that you can take them with you easily.
- ☐ Commit to finishing at least 1 book a week.
- ☐ Create a journal or notebook for recording your takeaways from these books.
- ☐ Keep a list of books that are suggested or that you come across that apply to your future or interests.

## CHAPTER 33

# GO PARTY!

———

*"People talk about work and play as separate things. But all of it is life. All of it is precious. Don't waste any of it doing something you don't want to do. And do all of it with the people you love."*

— RICHARD BRANSON

Aaron Rasmussen, the co-founder of MasterClass, shared a fun story and advice that most students would be happy to hear.

"I was a reckless 18-year-old sophomore. One day, we had this speaker come in to talk to my class. She was an executive at a local advertising agency. She said, 'Look I'm going to tell you something that your professor might not appreciate. It is the thing that helped me the most in business, and I think it will help you too. **Here it is: Go party.** Super drunk is not going to be fun. What you should try to do is meet and connect with people. This is the skill that you'll use in business every day."

I told myself challenge accepted. Please note that I was quite shy in my freshman year in college, too shy to enjoy parties in my free time. I started to challenge myself to hang out with people, understand others' perspectives, and learn more about them.

This is incredibly helpful because most people spend the majority of their day working with people, especially being an entrepreneur," Aaron explained. "Whether people will follow your vision or predicting whether you will keep or lose a customer all rely on your ability to connect and communicate with people. Therefore, it's incredibly important to spend your free time socializing."

To sum it up, practice your people skills at parties (and other places). And don't get wasted.

"Network like crazy!" Samuel Osei, the founder of an auto-repair company, gave me this advice during our interview. Samuel believes that connecting with as many students as possible on campus is one of the best things an entrepreneurial student can do. He even advocates for adding every student at your college to your social media. Why? Using his words, because a big following always helps.

It makes sense that a large network is especially helpful when starting a company. Samuel and many other entrepreneurs recommended to me that I should connect with people who are different than myself. Just ask people about their lives, talk to them, sit with someone during meal time. **The benefit is you will start to look at life from different perspectives.** College is probably a time that you will be surrounded by the widest range of diversity. Gaining a diverse perspective, and learning to think and experience from different viewpoints, is very beneficial.

In addition, Sam also thought that connecting with a large number of people is helpful for "finding talent." Once you get to know a good number of people on campus, what they are like, and what they are good at, the people you know start to turn into valuable resources. You will know enough good people to start a team, an organization, or a company with. Have you ever had a hard time to put together a good team? I know I have. And this is something I need to improve for sure. I do have many good friends outside of school, but I need to connect with more people on campus.

## ACTION CHECKLIST

- ☐ Go to a party or social gatherings every week to meet new people.
- ☐ Have deeper conversations with your friends to get to know them better.

☐ Reach out to interesting people on campus and meet them. (Could be the president of student government, a startup founder, and great computer engineer, or anyone you are interested in connecting with).

# CHAPTER 34

# START SOMETHING, ANYTHING

---

*"Screw it, let's do it."*

— RICHARD BRANSON

*"The only thing worse than starting something and failing … is not starting something."*

— SETH GODIN

This advice is the most frequently mentioned that I've come across from entrepreneurs while writing this book. When it comes to entrepreneurship, nothing can replace the experience of actually starting something.

More common advice: **College is the best time to start a**

**company because the risk is the lowest in college.** You don't need to worry about rent or any other costs. If you fail, you really don't lose anything other than time.

## STOP WAITING FOR PERMISSION

Kamal Ravikant once humorously said, "If I only did things I was qualified for I'd be pushing a broom somewhere." Many entrepreneurs told me to stop waiting for permission. Why? Because no one is going to give it to me. **Granted, maybe school trains us to wait for permission, but it doesn't work in the real world.** Students might tend to think, "Once I graduate, I will have the qualifications, and everything will magically work out." Well, it won't. Just like you probably won't find a perfect time that you feel 100% confident about starting a company or venture.

Mike Adams, the co-founder of MissionU, a program that is revolutionizing higher education, told me "'Stop waiting for permission' is the No.1 advice I will give to students." Mike hated his first job and that prompted him to start his own company. He said it was the best decision he has made. The feeling of, "Wow, I could actually start my own company" was a pivotal moment for him. Mike went on to say, "If I had that kind of moment sooner, I feel like I would be further along." The same thing applies to writing this book. If I was waiting for someone important to give me permission to write, we probably won't see this book for another 20 years.

## BUILD THE MUSCLE OF STARTING THINGS

Building and creating new things requires a special kind of muscle that is not used commonly when you are doing other activities. One of the main obstacles to starting anything is to overcome the inertia of creating something new and putting it into action. The other obstacles include keeping yourself motivated during tough times and not to giving up easily. These muscles can be developed by starting any organization including college clubs. Once you get good at it, starting things still won't be easy, but you know what challenges to expect and how to overcome them. **Many successful entrepreneurs started many smaller ventures before the famous companies that the public know**.

### *MARK ZUCKERBERG (CO-FOUNDER, FACEBOOK)*

While still in high school, he created an early version of the music software Pandora, which he called Synapse. At Harvard, he developed CourseMatch, which helped students choose their classes based on the course selections of other users. He also invented Facemash, which compared the pictures of two students on campus and allowed users to vote on which one was more attractive.

### JOE GEBBIA (CO-FOUNDER AIRBNB)

Joe started club basketball team at his college because he wanted to play in it. He was able to get the team started and schedule intramural games with other schools. While in college, Joe started a company CritBuns, which designed and sold a special kind of seat cushion for art students who often sit on the floor. Joe somehow convinced the school to purchase the CritBuns and give them out as graduation gift to each student. (I still can't imagine how he did it.)

### SETH GOLDMAN (CO-FOUNDER, HONEST TEA)

When I asked Seth how he decided to start a company, his response was, "I've always been pretty entrepreneurial since college. I started multiple things when I was at college and business school, which made starting a new company seem a lot more manageable."

### RICHARD BRANSON (FOUNDER, THE VIRGIN GROUP)

Richard's entrepreneurial journey started with the magazine he founded in high school. Later, he started his Virgin Empire by building Virgin Records, a company that disrupted the record label industry in a major way.

## REMEMBER: THE WORLD IS MADE UP
## BY PEOPLE NO SMARTER THAN YOU

*"When you grow up you tend to get told the world is the way it is and your life is just to live your life inside the world. Try not to bash into the walls too much. Try to have a nice family, have fun, save a little money. That's a very limited life. Life can be much broader once you discover one simple fact: Everything around you that you call life was made up by people that were no smarter than you and you can change it, you can influence it, you can build your own things that other people can use. Once you learn that, you'll never be the same again."*

— STEVE JOBS[1]

**From my personal experience, getting to know people who I once admired helped me to realize that they are also regular people.** They are not that much different or greater than I am. None were as untouchable or brilliant as the image that I created in my mind. Furthermore, a main reason that makes people seem amazing is precisely because they took the actions to do something amazing. They might have failed many times along the way, but the best way to learn is the learn by doing.

Entrepreneurs penetrate the fog of the unknown by testing their hypotheses through trial and error. Any entrepreneur (and any expert on cognition/learning) will tell you that practical knowledge is best developed by doing, not just thinking or planning.

## SCREW IT, LET'S DO IT

Richard Branson playfully wrote, "The staff at Virgin have a name for me. It is 'Dr. Yes.' They call me this because I won't say no. I find more reasons to do things than not to do them. My motto really is: 'Screw it — let's do it!' I will never say, 'I can't do this because I don't know how to.' I will give it a go. I won't let silly rules stop me. I will find a legal way around them. I tell my staff, 'If you want to do it, just do it.' That way we all benefit. The staff's work and ideas are valued and Virgin gains from their input and drive. I don't believe that that little word 'can't' should stop you. If you don't have the right experience to reach your goal, look for another way in."[2]

Richard Branson continued, "Today nothing is sure, and life is one long struggle. People have to make choices if they are to get anywhere. **The best lesson I learned was to just do it.** It doesn't matter what it is, or how hard it might seem, as the ancient Greek, Plato, said, 'The beginning is the most important part of any work.'"

Johann Wolfgang von Goethe said, "Whatever you can do or dream you can, begin it; Boldness has genius, power, and magic in it." START NOW.

## ACTION CHECKLIST

☐ Start a special project that you care about in the next month

☐ Start a student organization in the next 3 months

☐ Apply this "Two hours to build a business" hack in the next 3 months

    ☐ Come up with a problem and offer your solution

    ☐ Build a product landing page with a "buy now" button (1 hr)

    ☐ Create a Facebook Ad. If you want to go the extra mile, create a second ad with emphasis on a different benefit. Then do A/B test. (30 mins)

    ☐ Spend $30 on Facebook to run the ad (5 mins)

    ☐ Track and check the results. Are there real customers willing to pay for your product? What is the click through rate and conversion rate? You can find many other metrics. Then adjust and pivot your idea and product from there.

## CHAPTER 35

# FAIL FAST, FAIL FORWARD

——

*"One who fears failure limits his activities. Failure is only the opportunity to more intelligently begin again."*

—HENRY FORD

*"If you're doing your best, you won't have any time to worry about failure."*

— H. JACKSON BROWN, JR.

Mistakes and failures are inevitable in the journey of entrepreneurship. Actually, there are two things that lead to real failure:

1.    Being too afraid to fail, which results in not taking risks and

doing experiments. Ultimately, the company does not learn and pivot enough, and gets beaten by competitors.

2. Get beaten by failure and give up.

This leads to one conclusion: as long as you keep learning from your mistakes and failures, you are not failing. You are actually succeeding by moving closer to your target. This is a powerful hack because if you keep failing and learning, you will *definitely* succeed.

Ray Dalio is the founder of Bridgewater Associates, one of the largest hedge funds in the world. The secret to Dalio's success? The ability to acknowledge and systematically learn from his mistakes. "I've learned that everyone makes mistakes and has weaknesses," Dalio said in a missive outlining his life principles, "One of the most important things that differentiates people is their approach to handling them. I learned that there is an incredible beauty to mistakes, because each mistake was probably a reflection of something that I was doing wrong, so if I could figure out what that was, I could learn how to be more successful."[1]

## LEARNING FROM MISTAKES— EASIER SAID THAN DONE?

In *Mistakes Were Made (But Not by Me)*, social psychologist Elliot Aronson argues that our brains are constantly working hard to maintain a positive self-image, to believe that we're doing the right thing. These "ego-preserving blind-spots," Aronson writes, are pervasive: even prosecutors in police investigations with clear DNA evidence have difficulty accepting that "mistakes were made," for example. It's also not always clear exactly what "learning from your mistakes" means in practice. If you don't have a plan, you can easily end up just dwelling on what went wrong. This might be even worse than simply ignoring mistakes altogether—you don't learn anything, and you feel bad."[2]

Inspired by Dalio's principles and questions, ClearerThinking.org developed the following six-step process to help address a mistake:)[3]

1. What went wrong?
2. Have you made a mistake like this before?
3. What was the immediate cause of the problem?
4. What was the root cause of the problem?
5. What can you do to correct the problem in the short run?
6. What can you do to correct the problem in the long run?

## MINDSET IS THE MOST IMPORTANT THING

Start to view everything as an experiment and treat the results as experiment output so that you can learn something from each experience. Viewing failure as a learning experience takes practice, and I suppose that this is why so many entrepreneurs emphasize the importance of learning to fail.

When Sara Blakely was growing up, her father would often ask her the same question at dinnertime. **"What have you failed at this week?"** Blakely recalled in an interview on CNBC. "He would be disappointed if we didn't have many failures. My Dad, growing up, encouraged me and my brother to fail. The gift he was giving me is that failure is not trying versus the outcome. It's really allowed me to be much freer in trying things and spreading my wings in life." **Blakely's embrace of failure has helped make her the youngest self-made female billionaire in America.** Sara was selling fax machines door-to-door before she came up with the idea for Spanx, the body-shaping undergarments that have become a global sensation.

The co-founder of Instagram, Kevin Systrom, said in an interview, **"I think the best thing for any entrepreneur is failure."** Kevin is not just throwing out a nice quote. The failure of his first startup, Burbn, made him pay extra attention to customer feedback and ultimately identified the most successful feature of Burbn, which was photo sharing. From there, the idea for Instagram was born.

In September 2016, Elon Musk watched the failure of his latest attempt at landing his Space X Falcon 9 rocket; ice froze one of the legs and the entire rocket toppled over and exploded. That's another $60 million up in smoke. What was Elon's reaction? First, he tweeted "Well, at least the pieces were bigger this time!" Then, he posted a video of the explosion on Instagram. And later, he posted, "My best guess for 2016: ~70% landing success rate (so still a few more RUDs to go), then hopefully improving to ~90% in 2017." "RUD" stands for "Rapid Unscheduled Disassembly" which is another way of saying "it blew up." What can we learn from Elon happily blowing up his rockets? Most people would see this as an expensive failure. But **Elon is a master of learning by failing, and he expects to fail epically and often.**

**It doesn't cost Elon to fail as he builds it into his business model.** Each Falcon rocket is expected to be lost anyway, even if he wasn't testing how to land them. This one had already done its job of delivering an ocean monitoring satellite into orbit, which had already paid for the rocket. This year, there are another 10 to 20 Falcon rockets scheduled for take-off, each paid for by the companies or governments sending cargos into space. With the revenue stream secure, Elon focuses his time on how to test new innovations (like landing the returning rockets safely).

We've moved from the industrial age where product development and testing took place *before* delivery, to the technological age where product development and testing takes place *during* delivery. In the new paradigm, it's NOT testing that's far more expensive. As we can see, Elon is really walking his talk, "If things aren't failing, you are not innovating enough."[4]

## ACTION CHECKLIST

- ☐ Each day, ask yourself, "How did I fail?" Try more things and celebrate your failures.
- ☐ Whenever you feel bad or embarrassed about failing, which is natural, remind yourself to relax and learn. Cultivate this superpower of not feeling defeated when you fail.
- ☐ Read more about the failures of super successful people. This is the best way to reinforce your new belief around failure.

# CHAPTER 36

# HUSTLE LIKE CRAZY

—

*"Work twice as hard as anyone else."*

— ELON MUSK

*"If you want to be the best, you have to do things that others aren't willing to do"*

— MICHAEL PHELPS

"Mr. Musk, what is your advice to aspiring entrepreneurs?" Musk's answer did not even have a shade of romance. "Work like hell. You just have to put in 80 to 100 hours of work every week," he said. "If other people are putting in 40-hour work weeks, and you're putting in 100-hour work weeks, then, even if you're doing the same thing, you know that you will achieve in four months what it takes them a year to achieve."[1]

Most people who don't know Elon well, will not think of him as hardworking. Why? Because most people imagine he's the stereotypical technology genius. For heaven's sake, this dude taught himself rocket science! He is the real-world equivalent of the character Iron Man, Tony Stark. You might think his success must be the result of an inhuman IQ. Without a doubt, Elon is smart, but his work ethic is also unmatched by most entrepreneurs in the world.

This story demonstrates what he meant by "working super hard." When Elon started his company with his brother, "Instead of renting an apartment, we rented an office and slept on a couch. We showered at the YMCA. We were so held up we only had one computer. The website was up during the day, and I was coding at night. Seven days a week, all the time. I sort of briefly had a girlfriend at that time. In order to be with me, she had to be in the office." Musk continued with this advice, "Work hard every single waking hour. In particular if you are starting a company."[2]

Another story of hard work paying off in about the man who just became the wealthiest person in the world, Jeff Bezos. Amazon CEO Jeff Bezos' high school classmates gave up when he decided he wanted to be valedictorian. Why? Because Jeff always had a relentless work ethic. A former classmate told *Wired* that once Jeff made it clear that he intended to be high school valedictorian, "Everyone else understood they were working for second place." The early days at Amazon were characterized by working 12-hour days, seven days a week, and being up until 3 a.m. to get books shipped. Now that Amazon is a giant success, Jeff continues to personally email teams about customer service issues and has them present directly to him about how they're going to solve them, according to an excerpt from Brad Stone's book, *The Everything Store*."[3]

Dallas Mavericks owner Mark Cuban didn't take a vacation for seven years while starting his first business. On a similar note, Gary Vaynerchuk, the founder of VaynerMedia and Wine Library, worked at his father's wine store and Wine Library for about ten years in his twenties without any vacation, even on the weekends. Outside of the business world, Michael Phelps, the guy who won 23 Olympics gold medals, never took a day off in five years during his most intense training period. That's right, not even Christmas or his birthday.

I fear that hard work is normally ignored because people just love to credit success to luck or talent, especially in the entrepreneurial world. However, your hustle and hard work cannot be overlooked. Even if you do have the IQ of Elon Musk.

Just like most Americans think the Chinese are good at math or school in general, they ignore the fact that students in China spend at least two more hours studying every day, starting in primary school. I still remember my amazement when I first came to the States for high school. I was so surprised to see how little many students studied. Then I realized that the amount of time Chinese high school students study was literally a foreign concept for my American classmates. Most of them could not even think of being in school from 8 a.m. to 10 p.m. (14 hours), plus homework. Just as most people in the US have not even thought of working 100+ hours a week.

Interestingly, my original standard for hard work was shattered when I interviewed my mentor for this book. My mentor Ari Rastegar, started his private equity firm with a focus on real estate two years ago, and now the company has assets under management for over 1 billion dollars. Ari believes hard work is, hands down, the most important thing for an entrepreneur. He went on a passionate rant for minutes. He even said that, if you are a student entrepreneur and you work for less than 100 hours a week (including school work), it's not going to cut it. Ari worked full time during college with multiple jobs, such as pizza delivering and tutoring, to make the ends meet.

During law school, Ari started a real estate company. "I started a construction company with $3000 from my old college buddy's father and I used $3000 of my scholarship money. I bought a little piece of land that cost me like $2,100. I was school, so I hired a contractor to come help me build these little houses. I got to the building site at five o'clock in the morning, and I left sites around 11am. I made all my classes after twelve."

He also scheduled all his classes on two days, so that he had chunks of time to work on the business. He worked for more than 100 hours a week, and never had a weekend off during that time. In the end, Ari *still passed* the bar exam. And he sold his company for millions of dollars two years after graduation.

## ACTION CHECKLIST

- ☐ Choose hustle over excuses.
- ☐ Find people who hustle and surround yourself with those people.
- ☐ For the next 2 weeks, start to work for 80 hours or more a week. See how it feels.
- ☐ Work on improving your productivity (reference to the chapter on planning and time management).

# CHAPTER 37

# CREATE OVERNIGHT SUCCESS

——

*"I'm convinced that about half of what separates successful entrepreneurs from the non — successful ones is pure perseverance."*

— STEVE JOBS

*"It takes 20 years to make an overnight success."*

— EDDIE CANTOR

Patience = To be willing to wait longer to achieve your goal
Perseverance = Patience with perspiration
Resilience = Perseverance through failure

Patience, perseverance and resilience are three different shades of the same quality. Some people have one or two, but not all three. Some people can persevere, but are not patient. Some are patient, but not resilient. Strengthen all three, and you have **the key quality shared by all great entrepreneurs: Endurance.**[1]

As young people, we often overlook irreplaceable importance of putting our head down and working. Nothing can replace the time and energy invested over a long period of time and the wisdom gained from that. Spending years on improving your "deserve-it factor," your ideas, and your products might not be the fastest way, but this is the surest way to achieve greatness.

## PATIENCE

In 1958, at 48 years old, Momofuku invented instant noodles. Not satisfied with his first invention, he kept working at making noodles cheaper and easier to cook, and, finally, 13 years later in 1971 at 61 years old, he created Pot Noodles.

Over the next 30 years, his noodles have grown in popularity worldwide. **Over 100 billion servings of instant noodles are now sold every year.** That's 15 for every human on earth. In a national poll, the Japanese people voted instant noodle as the greatest Japanese invention of the 20th Century.

## PERSEVERANCE

How long does it take to create an overnight success? For John Hanke, it took him 20 years to create *Pokémon Go*. In 2016, the *Pokémon Go* app broke all records, with 10 million+ downloads in the first week, exceeding Twitter in daily active users, and with higher average user time than Facebook, Snapchat, Instagram, and WhatsApp.

How did John Hanke create such a massive overnight craze? **He leveled ten times to reach *Pokémon Go*.**

**1st Level up**: In 1996, while still a student, John co-created the very first MMO (massively multiplayer online game). He sold the game to move on to a bigger passion: mapping the world.

**2nd Level up:** In 2000, John launched *Keyhole* to come up with a way to create the first online, GPS-linked 3D aerial map of the world.

**3rd Level up:** In 2004, Google bought *Keyhole* and with John's help, turned Keyhole into what is now *Google Earth*. That's when John decided to focus at creating GPS-based games.

**4th Level up:** John ran the Google Geo team from 2004 to 2010, creating *Google Maps* and *Google Street View*. During this time, he collected the team that would later create *Pokémon Go*.

**5th Level up:** In 2010, John launched Niantic Labs as a start-up funded by Google to create a game layer on maps.

**6th Level up:** In 2012, John then created Niantic's first geo-based MMO, *Ingress*, John explained, "In the case of *Ingress*, the activity is layered on top of the real world and on your phone."

**7th Level up:** In 2014, Google and the Pokémon Company teamed up for an April Fools' Day joke, which allowed viewers to find Pokémon creatures on Google maps. It was a viral hit, and got John thinking the idea could be turned into a real game.

**8th Level up:** John decided to build *Pokémon Go* on the user-generated meeting points created by players of *Ingress*.

**9th Level up:** John raised $25 million from Google, Nintendo, the Pokémon Company, and other investors to grow the team from Dec 2015 to Feb 2016.

**10th Level up:** John and his team launched *Pokémon Go* on July 6, 2016, in the USA, Australia, and New Zealand. Since its launch, Nintendo's share price has risen to $12 billion, and the app is already generating over $2 million daily in in-app purchases, making it an overnight phenomenon.[2]

## RESILIENCE

By 2004, Elon Musk became the co-founder of Tesla Motors, SpaceX, and a chairman at SolarCity. Musk infamously noted, "My proceeds from the PayPal acquisition were $180 million. I put $100 million in SpaceX, $70m in Tesla, and $10m in Solar City. I had to borrow money for rent." While most individuals would spend their money and become more risk-averse after receiving a nine-figure check, Musk used all of his money to the point at which he was in debt just so he was able to service his hunger to expand as an entrepreneur. At one point this became no joking matter, Elon was getting loans left and right, and had no income to pay them back.

Things got so bad in 2008 that Tesla would have to be shut down in 24 hours if not enough money was raised. Elon teared up when an interviewer asked him about the tough situation in 2008. Elon said, "Having a business is like having a child. How can you tell the child there is no food?" There is no doubt that even the superhuman Elon Musk has gone through tremendous hardship to be where he is today. And the true story is far from the appearance of an overnight success.

## ACTION CHECKLIST

☐ List the ways you can make yourself stronger.
☐ List the ways you can improve your product.

☐ Read about the failures and patience of successful entrepreneurs. Do this daily.

## CHAPTER 38

# BUILD A REAL
# NETWORK

———

*"You can get all you want in life, if you help enough people get what they want."*

— ZIG ZIGLAR

Many people are turned off by the topic of networking. They think it feels slimy, inauthentic. Go figure. Picture the consummate networker: the high-energy fast talker who collects as many business cards as he can at evening networking mixers. As Reid Hoffman, co-founder of LinkedIn puts it, "These people are drunk on networking Kool-Aid and await a potential nasty social and professional hangover." Luckily, building and strengthening your network doesn't have to be like this. Old-school "networkers" are transactional; they focus on what they can get from you. The new way of networking is "relational."[1]

Think about some of your happiest memories. Were you alone? Or were you surrounded by friends or family? Think about some of your most adventurous, stimulating experiences. Building relationships should be fun and rewarding. I certainly find that relationships and people are the most beautiful parts of my memories. And this is the main reason I spend time and energy on creating more meaningful connections.

## NETWORKING HACKS[2]

The following are some of the best ways to build relationships from Reid Hoffman plus some lessons from my personal experiences.

### 1. EMPATHIZE AND HELP FIRST

Building a genuine relationship with another person depends on (at least) two things. The first is seeing the world from the other person's perspective. No one knows this better than the skilled entrepreneur. Entrepreneurs succeed when they make stuff people will pay money for, which means understanding the needs and desires of others.

The second requirement is thinking about how you can help

and collaborate with the other person rather than thinking about what you can get from him or her. When you come into contact with a successful person, it's natural to immediately think, "What can this person do for me?" If you were to have a chance meeting with someone famous or powerful, we can't blame you for thinking about how you could get your photo taken. However, people like to receive. **And reciprocity is one of the most powerful tools you can use.**

As you meet your friends and new people, shift from asking yourself the very natural question of "What's in it for me?" And ask instead, "What's in it for us?" To make it even better, how different would it be if you approach each person with the question in your mind, "**How can I add value to you?**" This is the question I ask often when interacting with people I want to connect with. It's easy because I generally like, appreciate, or care about people I want to connect with.

**This hack works wonders.** I can't tell you how well it works. This question is the No.1 reason why I've been able to connect with some successful and powerful people. Even though sometimes the value I add is a simple recommendation to a person, a book, or a system that might be helpful to a problem they face. Or even simpler, a thoughtful thank you note with some sincere compliments. **People can feel your attention and mindset in seconds.**

This is the FIRST thing that you must do in order to be successful at networking. All the rest comes after this.

## 2. BE A COOL PERSON

This is a hack, not a shortcut. To many people just try to reach out and connect with cool, interesting, and successful people. However, why would those people want to build a relationship with them if they aren't cool, interesting, and successful? People need to remember you for something. What do you want that something to be? It can be a mixture of your humility, hunger, cool experiences, impressive achievements, pleasant personality, and more. This goes back to spending more time on building your "deserve it" factor.

## 3. KEEP IN TOUCH

There is nothing worse than receiving an out-of-the-blue email from someone you haven't spoken to in three years: "Hey, we met a few years ago at that conference. Listen, I'm looking for a job in the marketing world — do you know anyone hiring?" You think, 'Oh, I see, you only contact me when you need something.'"

Reid has more recommendations regarding keeping in touch:

- **You're probably not nagging.** A common fear people have about staying in touch and following up is that the other person will perceive you as annoying and pushy. Do you come off as needy if you follow up multiple times? Well, it depends. But usually not. Keep following up politely if you don't get an answer — and try to mix up the message, the gift, the approach. With the amount of noise polluting people's inbox, it's common for emails to get buried. Until you hear "No," you haven't been turned down.

- **Try to add value.** Check in with someone when you can offer something more than a generic greeting or personal update. Examples: you see his name in the news, read an article he wrote or was quoted in, or know a qualified candidate for a position he is trying to fill. It's unimpressive to send a note simply asking, "How are you?"

- **If you're worried about seeming too personal, couch staying-in-touch as massive action.** Does it feel weird reaching out to a high school classmate you haven't spoken to in years? Here's a tip: Couch your initial getting-back-in-touch action as part of a more generic process: "I'm trying to reconnect with old classmates from high school. How are you?"

- **One lunch is worth dozens of emails.** A one-hour lunch with a person creates a bond that would take dozens of electronic communications. When you can, meet in person.

- **Social media.** To stay in touch passively, use social media. As you push one-to-many updates out to your network and followers, if someone you know wants to respond, he or she can. But there's no obligation. I personally use social media a lot to stay contact with people. I also use it to see what is going on in their lives before contacting them for important issues.

## 3. BE A BRIDGE

A good way to help people is to introduce them to people and experiences they wouldn't otherwise be able to access. In other words, straddle different communities/social circles and then be the bridge that your friends can walk over. Make sure to get permission from both sides first. This tool is especially useful for college students because it is a relatively easy way to add value to the other person.

## 4. SET UP AN "INTERESTING PEOPLE FUND"

You might be nodding your head at the importance of staying in touch. But will you actually follow through? Enacting behavioral change isn't easy. When you actually have to do the thing you know is important, it's tempting to push it off for another day.

In addition to a monetary amount, also set a time amount. On a given month, how much time and money are you allocated toward building your network? Schedule time on your calendar for keeping in touch with your network or going to lunch with new contacts.

## 5. NAVIGATE STATUS DYNAMICS WHEN DEALING WITH POWERFUL PEOPLE

If you want to maintain relationships with busy, powerful people, you have to pay special attention to the role of status. As college students, it is likely that most people we want to connect with are a lot more powerful than we are. The following guidelines are crucial to starting a relationship with successful people:

- **Never be late.** Tardiness is the classic power move because it says, "My time is more valuable than yours, so it's okay for you to wait for me." Think about it: Would you allow yourself to be late to a meeting with the President? Certainly not.
- **Do what is more convenient for the other person.** Whether it is the meeting location, meeting time, or other factors, always be accommodating. If you want to build a relationship with someone of higher status, learn to be flexible. The social terrain at the highest levels of power and influence can be treacherous. A little bit of conscientiousness in this department goes a long way.

## ACTION CHECKLIST

- ☐ Find 10 people you want to connect with.
- ☐ Reach out to them with a mindset of how can you add value.
- ☐ Schedule some time and set aside some money to work on these relationships.

☐ Apply the hacks mentioned above in as many relationships possible.

CHAPTER 39

# TASTE THE STARTUP WORLD

———

*"If you can't feed a team with two pizzas, it's too large."*

— JEFF BEZOS

At this stage, you probably have realized that startups and big corporations are different creatures. They are different in the ways they operate, hire, solve problems, prioritize, and more. Therefore, working or interning in a startup is an important hack in your entrepreneurial journey. That "taste" can make all the difference for you. When you work in a startup, all the entrepreneurship concepts you have learned, such as the importance of testing, MVP, customer development, and pivoting will suddenly come alive. There is no better way to learn than direct experience.

Before my senior year, I had a great internship experience at MasterClass, a two-year old company that is revolutionizing online education by giving people access to learn from the "best of the best" in different fields.

First and foremost, the culture at MasterClass was amazing. In contrast to the typical bureaucracy, the culture is very outcome-driven and collaborative. People have the freedom to achieve key results, regardless of methods or time input. As a result, I saw many mission-driven people motivated to accomplish the results and beyond. In addition, each person has the opportunity to make a difference because of the team size and culture. No one felt like a cog in a big machine. Instead, people are always thinking about a better way of doing things and discussing those ideas, because every idea had the potential to make a difference.

The organization is intentionally flat, meaning there was not a strong sense of difference in ranks. This enabled collaboration and interaction between the senior directors and new interns like me. This reinforced the culture of being outcome-driven and collaborative. It was cool to be able to sit down next to the COO, CEO, or other senior management people at lunch and ask questions.

It was extremely cool and eye-opening to experience the philosophy of "test everything" was. At MasterClass, we took "test everything" literally. We tested to get feedback on potential instructors, trailers, classes, advertising, website design, and more. Whenever an important question arose, the default thinking was "let's test this," instead of arguing who's right or simply listening to the managers.

As icing on the cake, there were unlimited supplies of healthy snacks and drinks, many fun social events, and free catered meals.

In summary, I learned a ton from my time at MasterClass about entrepreneurship and marketing. Better yet, I made some great friends and worked with some of the most amazing managers. In the end, I felt like a part of a big family.

Go experience the startup world with your own eyes. You won't regret it. By the way, a lack of internship positions on the career page should never stop you from reaching out to a startup that you're interested in working with.

## ACTION CHECKLIST

- ☐ Identify 10 local startups you would like to intern with.
- ☐ Reach out to the startups and ask about internship opportunities.
- ☐ Identify 10 major startups you want to intern at during the summer.
- ☐ Apply for the internships early with your best effort.

☐ Find the appropriate people on your campus to talk to about internships. They may know companies that are looking for people just like you. Or, if the companies you contacted need help setting up the internship, you'll have the information at hand.

# CHAPTER 40

# WRITE A BOOK

___

*Whatever you can do or dream you can, begin it; Boldness has genius, power, and magic in it.*

— JOHANN WOLFGANG VON GOETHE

*It always seems impossible until it's done.*

— NELSON MANDELA

Alright, I am not recommending writing a book because I did it. Instead, I am doing it because I realized through my experience that this might be the best exercise for any aspiring entrepreneur. During the book interviews with successful entrepreneurs, all the interviewees **loved** the idea of writing a book as a training in entrepreneurship. The book should be a nonfiction book that teaches people something, and it can be on anything you are passionate about. Choose a field, dig deep, interview experts, and create a book that adds value to others.

Here are some reason why you should write a book:

1.  Creating best practices for starting something big without waiting for permission. Most people wait for permission to do something awesome. The permissions can be a diploma, a great job, a brilliant idea, or support from loved ones. Once we get in the permission-seeking mindset, it's likely that we will delay starting something indefinitely. No one will give you the permission to start a company or writing a book. People may ask, "Who do you think you are?" Well, you can't become "somebody" unless you do something cool.

2.  You will feel damn good about yourself after writing a book. You will start to wonder, "What else is possible?" This pride and confidence can lead you to more and more entrepreneurial ventures.

3.  You won't feel like doing it. Writing a book can't be done overnight, and in that way, it's just like building a business. It takes months of hard work, you'll get plenty of practice overcoming resistance and procrastination. You won't feel like doing the work most of the time, even though you want the final product. It takes planning, patience, discipline, resilience, and perseverance to push through and get it finished. All these are also elements necessary for building a successful company.

4.  You'll have a great opportunity to connect with more successful people. When you are writing a book about a certain subject,

it's a lot easier to get accomplished experts in that field to talk to you, even though you are still a student. This is one of the best ways to build your skill in building a relationship with accomplished people.

5. You establish expertise in whatever field you wrote about. If the book is related to your career aspiration, the book will almost guarantee a job offer.

6. Finally, having a published a book is COOL. Well, it's more than cool. It's cool, memorable, interesting, attention-grabbing, and it helps you stand out. Did you know there are about 20 million college students in the US alone?[1] Out of the 20 million, only about 30 students publish nonfictional books each year. Do the math, 120 nonfiction book authors in four years then divide by 20 million, that's 0.0006% of the college student populations. It's almost impossible to build a resume that puts you in the top 0.0006% of the applicants.

## ACTION CHECKLIST

☐ Identify books, websites, or programs that will guide you through the book writing process.

☐ Check out *Signal Class* for publishing resources specifically for college students.

☐ Post on social media to let everyone know that you are writing a book. This pressure and attention from friends will give you some extra motivation to keep going when things get tough.

☐ Start writing a book.

# ACKNOWLEDGMENTS

---

This book would not have been possible without the people mentioned below. To say the least, I am standing on the shoulders of giants. To be more precise, I am outrageously blessed to have these people in my life. Thank you for shaping who I am and who I am becoming. There are many other people I want to acknowledge here but couldn't due to space limitations. My deepest gratitude and love goes to all of you. I love you, thank you!

*Family: for your unconditional love and support*
Mom (Xiangying Zou), Dad (Shengyue Liu), and other family members. Special thanks to my parents for offering me the love and freedom to literally explore the world. By the way, the name they gave me (my real legal name) is Zhuoyun Liu, though I use "Antonia" in English-speaking countries.

The extended family that includes Shanna and Greg Parry, Donny and Jackie Epstein, Mari Vasan, Stephanie Wu, Paula and Ben Haven, Silian Chen, and Shu Tan.

*Editors: for helping me create a real book*
Jennifer Taylor (the developmental editor who played an instrumental role), Erica Whalen, Myles Parker, and Zachary Tousignant.

*Mentors and teachers: for guiding and shaping who I am*
Tony Robbins (who has profoundly shaped who I am today), Ari Rastegar, Scott Andrews, Arthur Kerry Brown, Anzhi Chen, Rich Fryling, David Shaner, Nanrong Xu, Yi Zuo, Bei He, Mike Wang, and Jon Frank.

*Influences: for influencing the way I look at the world*
Tim Ferriss, Richard Branson, Cal Newport, Jay Abraham, Ray Dalio, Gary Vaynerchuk, Seth Godin, Oprah Winfrey, Bill Clinton, Paulo Coelho, Jack Ma, and Elon Musk.

*Friends: for making the journey so much more joyful and meaningful*
Indra Acharya and Desmond Ferrell, Reed Howard and Laura Chant, Kavi Patel, Ariel Zhang, Adam Siddiq, Molham Krayem, Frankie Mirandes, Miriam Magalhaes, Stephanie Bridwell, Kim Keating, and my other Georgetown, Cape Cod Academy,

Chengdu Foreign Language School, and Tony Robbins
Community friends

*New Degree Press team: for making this book possible by
providing incredible faith and encouragement when most
needed*
Eric Koester, Brian Bies, and Anastasia Armendariz

*All the people that I interviewed for this book: for giving me
the insights and wisdom that guided this book from start
to finish*
Aaron Rasmussen, Ari Rastegar, Cal Newport, Seth Goldman,
Willard Barth, Bill Carmody, Katie Meyler, Samuel Osei, David
Shaner, Nathan Chan, Liz Wessel, Mike Adams, and more.

# APPENDIX

---

## *INTRODUCTION*

1. "Amway Global Entrepreneurship Report." *Amway*, Amway, 2016, globalnewsassets.amway.com/501484/ager_2016_publication.pdf?r=1600.

## *CHAPTER 2*

1. Robbins, Anthony. "Rapid Planning Method Workbook." *Tony Robbi*ns, www.tonyrobbins.com/pdfs/Workbook-Time-of-your-Life.pdf.

2. Hyatt, Michael, and Daniel Harkavy. *Living Forward: a Proven Plan to Stop Drifting and Get the Life You Want.* Baker Books, Baker Publishing Group, 2016.

3. Hyatt, Michael, and Daniel Harkavy. *Living Forward: a*

*Proven Plan to Stop Drifting and Get the Life You Want.* Baker Books, Baker Publishing Group, 2016.

## CHAPTER 3

1. Branson, Richard. "Richard Branson: My Six Tips for Every Young Entrepreneur." *Virgin*, 27 Apr. 2017, www.virgin.com/ entrepreneur/richard-branson-my-six-tips-for-every-young-entrepreneur.
2. Gillett, Rachel. "Elon Musk's First Wife Explains What It Takes to Find Your Passion." *Business Insider*, Business Insider, 11 Sept. 2015, www.businessinsider.com/ elon-musks-first-wife-explains-what-it-takes-to-find-your-passion-2015-9.

## CHAPTER 4

1. Haden, Jeff. "Do What You Love? Screw That." *Inc.com*, Inc., 14 Nov. 2012, www.inc.com/jeff-haden/worst-career-advice-do-what-you-love.html?nav=pop.
2. Newport, Cal. So Good They Can't Ignore You: Why Skills Trump Passion in the Quest for Work You Love. Grand Central Publishing, 2012.
3. Milord, Joseph. "Peter Thiel Shares His 9 Most Essential Pieces Of Advice For Generation-Y." *Elite Daily*, Elite Daily, 11 Sept. 2017, www.elitedaily.com/money/entrepreneurship/ peter-thiels-9-pieces-advice-entrepreneurs-generation-y.

## CHAPTER 5

1. Hoffman, Reid, and Ben Casnocha. The Start-up of you: adapt to the future, invest in yourself, and transform your career. New York, Crown Business, 2012.

2. Hoffman, Reid, and Ben Casnocha. The Start-up of you: adapt to the future, invest in yourself, and transform your career. New York, Crown Business, 2012.

3. Hoffman, Reid, and Ben Casnocha. The Start-up of you: adapt to the future, invest in yourself, and transform your career. New York, Crown Business, 2012.

4. Hoffman, Reid, and Ben Casnocha. The Start-up of you: adapt to the future, invest in yourself, and transform your career. New York, Crown Business, 2012.

## CHAPTER 6

1. Ferriss, Timothy. Tools of Titans: the Tactics, Routines, and Habits of Billionaires, Icons, and World-Class Performers. Houghton Mifflin Harcourt, 2017.

## CHAPTER 9

1. Wagner, Eric T. "Five Reasons 8 Out Of 10 Businesses Fail." Forbes, Forbes Magazine, 2 Sept. 2015, www.forbes.com/sites/ericwagner/2013/09/12/five-reasons-8-out-of-10-businesses-fail/.

2. Hamilton, Roger. *Entrepreneur Inspiration Edition 2*. 2016. E-book. http://rogerjameshamilton.com/entrepreneurinspiration/

## CHAPTER 10

1. Hamilton, Roger. *Entrepreneur Inspiration Edition* 2. 2016. E-book. http://rogerjameshamilton.com/ entrepreneurinspiration/

2. Gibson, Megan. "Mark Zuckerberg's Advice for Young People Who Want to Change the World." Time, Time, 6 Mar. 2015, time.com/3735363/mark-zuckerberg-young-people/.

3. Elkins, Kathleen. "Facebook's Mark Zuckerberg Shares His Best Advice for Aspiring Entrepreneurs." CNBC, CNBC, 17 Aug. 2016, www.cnbc.com/2016/08/17/facebooks-mark-zuckerberg-shares-his-best-advice-for-aspiring-entrepreneurs.html.

## CHAPTER 12

1. Hamilton, Roger. *Entrepreneur Inspiration Edition* 2. 2016. E-book. http://rogerjameshamilton.com/ entrepreneurinspiration/

## CHAPTER 13

1. Manson, Mark. "The Subtle Art of Not Giving a Fuck." *Mark Manson*, 24 July 2017, markmanson.net/not-giving-a-fuck.

2. Manson, Mark. "The Subtle Art of Not Giving a Fuck." *Mark Manson*, 24 July 2017, markmanson.net/not-giving-a-fuck.

## CHAPTER 14

1. Robbins, Anthony, and Peter Mallouk. *Unshakeable: Your Financial Freedom Playbook*. Simon & Schuster, 2017.

2. Robbins, Anthony, and Peter Mallouk. *Unshakeable: Your Financial Freedom Playbook*. Simon & Schuster, 2017.

## CHAPTER 15

1. Ferriss, Timothy. Tools of Titans: the Tactics, Routines, and Habits of Billionaires, Icons, and World-Class Performers. Houghton Mifflin Harcourt, 2017.
2. Roche, Julia La. "Ray Dalio: More than Anything Else, I Attribute My Success to One Thing." *Yahoo!* Finance, Yahoo!, 20 May 2016, finance.yahoo.com/news/ray-dalio-featured-in-dr-normal-rosenthal-book-super-mind-152727852.html.
3. Ferriss, Timothy. Tools of Titans: the Tactics, Routines, and Habits of Billionaires, Icons, and World-Class Performers. Houghton Mifflin Harcourt, 2017.

## CHAPTER 16

1. Pressfield, Steven. The War of Art: Break through the Blocks and Win Your Inner Creative Battles. Black Irish Entertainment, 2002.
2. Pressfield, Steven. The War of Art: Break through the Blocks and Win Your Inner Creative Battles. Black Irish Entertainment, 2002.

## CHAPTER 17

1. "On the Shortness of Life Quotes by Seneca." *Seneca*, Greatreads, www.goodreads.com/work/quotes/1374471-de-brevitate-vitae.

2.  Ferriss, Timothy. Tools of Titans: the Tactics, Routines, and Habits of Billionaires, Icons, and World-Class Performers. Houghton Mifflin Harcourt, 2017.

3.  Team Tony, *Time of Your Life Workbook*. https://www.tony-robbins.com/pdfs/Workbook-Time-of-your-Life.pdf

4.  Ferriss, Timothy. Tools of Titans: the Tactics, Routines, and Habits of Billionaires, Icons, and World-Class Performers. Houghton Mifflin Harcourt, 2017.

## CHAPTER 18

1.  McSpadden, Kevin. *"Science: You Now Have a Shorter Attention Span Than a Goldfish."* Time, Time, 14 May 2015, time.com/3858309/attention-spans-goldfish/.

2.  Newport, Cal. Deep Work: Rules for Focused Success in a Distracted World. Grand Central Publishing, 2016.

3.  Newport, Cal. Deep Work: Rules for Focused Success in a Distracted World. Grand Central Publishing, 2016.

4.  Newport, Cal. Deep Work: Rules for Focused Success in a Distracted World. Grand Central Publishing, 2016.

## CHAPTER 21

1.  Feloni, Richard. "A Simple 3-Step Exercise to Figure out What's Holding You Back from Success." *Business Insider*, Business Insider, 24 Apr. 2015, www.businessinsider.com/tim-ferriss-on-exercise-to-overcome-fears-2015-4.

2.  Ferriss, Timothy. The 4-Hour Workweek: Escape 9-5, Live Anywhere, and Join the New Rich. Harmony Books, 2012.

## CHAPTER 22

1. Ries, Eric. The Lean Startup: How Today's Entrepreneurs Use Continuous Innovation to Create Radically Successful Businesses. Crown Business, 2014.

## CHAPTER 23

1. Ellsberg, Michael. The Education of Millionaires: Everything You Won't Learn in College about How to Be Successful. Portfolio/Penguin, 2012.
2. Abraham, Jay. Abraham 101. Jay Abraham.

## CHAPTER 24

1. Hamilton, Roger. Entrepreneur Inspiration Edition 2. 2016. E-book. http://rogerjameshamilton.com/entrepreneurinspiration/

## CHAPTER 25

1. Team Tony, "HOW TO GET WHAT YOU WANT." Tony Robbins. https://www.tonyrobbins.com/mind-meaning/how-to-get-what-you-want/?utm_source=-facebook&utm_campaign=Editorial&utm_medi-um=social&utm_content=How%20Get%20You%20Want
2. Team Tony, "HOW TO GET WHAT YOU WANT." Tony Robbins. https://www.tonyrobbins.com/mind-meaning/how-to-get-what-you-want/?utm_source=-facebook&utm_campaign=Editorial&utm_medi-

um=social&utm_content=How%20Get%20You%20
Want

## CHAPTER 26

1.  Ferriss, Timothy. Tools of Titans: the Tactics, Routines, and Habits of Billionaires, Icons, and World-Class Performers. Houghton Mifflin Harcourt, 2017.
2.  Team Tony. "Tony Robbins Priming Exercise, Learn How It Works!" Tonyrobbins.com, Tony Robbins, www.tonyrobbins.com/ask-tony/priming/.
3.  Elrod, Hal. The Miracle Morning: the Not-so-Obvious Secret Guaranteed to Transform Your Life before 8AM. Hal Elrod International, Inc., 2016.

## CHAPTER 27

1.  Team Tony, "PEER ELEVATION." Tony Robbins. https://www.tonyrobbins.com/mind-meaning/peer-communities/

## CHAPTER 28

1.  Hamilton, Roger. Entrepreneur Inspiration Edition 2. 2016. E-book. http://rogerjameshamilton.com/entrepreneurinspiration/
2.  Dalio, Ray. Principles Life and Work. Simon and Schuster, 2017.

## CHAPTER 29

1. Ginsberg, Leah. "Mark Zuckerberg, Richard Branson and Mark Cuban All Agree This One Habit Is Key to Success." *CNBC*, CNBC, 28 May 2017, www.cnbc.com/2017/05/28/mark-zuckerberg-and-richard-branson-exercise-is-key-to-success.html?view=story&%24DEVICE%24=native-android-mobile.

2. Goldman, Seth. "6 Reasons Why Running Is the Perfect Sport for Entrepreneurs." Inc.com, Inc., 9 Mar. 2017, www.inc.com/seth-goldman/6-reasons-why-running-is-the-perfect-sport-for-entrepreneurs.html.

## CHAPTER 30

1. Lopez, Thai. The-67-Steps Program. http://www.the67steps.com

## CHAPTER 31

1. Branson, Richard. "Richard Branson Explains How to Master the Art of Reading between the Lines." *Business Insider*, Business Insider, 29 Oct. 2015, www.businessinsider.com/richard-branson-how-to-be-an-effective-listener-2015-10.

2. Branson, Richard. The Virgin Way: Everything I Know about Leadership. Portfolio Hardcover, 2014.

3. Branson, Richard. The Virgin Way: Everything I Know about Leadership. Portfolio Hardcover, 2014.

## CHAPTER 32

1. Merle, Andrew. "The Reading Habits of Ultra-Successful People." *The Huffington Post*, TheHuffingtonPost.com, 14 Apr. 2016, www.huffingtonpost.com/andrew-merle/the-reading-habits-of-ult_b_9688130.html.

2. Merle, Andrew. "The Reading Habits of Ultra-Successful People." *The Huffington Post*, TheHuffingtonPost.com, 14 Apr. 2016, www.huffingtonpost.com/andrew-merle/the-reading-habits-of-ult_b_9688130.html.

## CHAPTER 34

1. Gurteen, David. "Everything Was Made up by People That Were No Smarter than You by Steve Jobs (Gurteen Knowledge)." *Gurteen.com*, www.gurteen.com/gurteen/gurteen.nsf/id/no-smarter-than-you.

2. Branson, Richard. The Virgin Way: Everything I Know about Leadership. Portfolio Hardcover, 2014.

## CHAPTER 35

1. Whittlestone, Jess. "Learning from mistakes can change your fortune-or earn you one." *Quartz*, Quartz, 18 Mar. 2015, qz.com/363628/learning-from-mistakes-can-change-your-fortune-or-earn-you-one/. Accessed 26 Sept. 2017.

2. Whittlestone, Jess. "Learning from mistakes can change your fortune-or earn you one." *Quartz*, Quartz, 18 Mar. 2015, qz.com/363628/learning-from-mistakes-can-change-your-fortune-or-earn-you-one/. Accessed 26 Sept. 2017.

3.  Whittlestone, Jess. "Learning from mistakes can change your fortune-or earn you one." *Quartz*, Quartz, 18 Mar. 2015, qz.com/363628/learning-from-mistakes-can-change-your-fortune-or-earn-you-one/. Accessed 26 Sept. 2017.

4.  Hamilton, Roger. *Entrepreneur Inspiration Edition* 2. 2016. E-book. http://rogerjameshamilton.com/entrepreneurinspiration/

## CHAPTER 36

1.  Elon Musk: Work twice as hard as others. Vator. https://www.youtube.com/watch?v=GtaxU6DZvLs

2.  Elon Musk — Work ethics, Principles, Attitude, Failure — Pearls of Advice. ImagE Native. https://www.youtube.com/watch?v=NU7W7qe2RoA

3.  Taube, Aaron. "17 People Whose Incredible Work Ethic Paid Off." *Business Insider*, Business Insider, 5 Dec. 2014, www.businessinsider.com/17-hard-working-successful-people-2014-12#amazon-ceo-jeff-bezos-high-school-classmates-gave-up-when-he-decided-he-wanted-to-be-valedictorian-5.

## CHAPTER 37

1.  Hamilton, Roger. *Entrepreneur Inspiration Edition* 2. 2016. E-book. http://rogerjameshamilton.com/entrepreneurinspiration/

2.  Hamilton, Roger. *Entrepreneur Inspiration Edition* 2. 2016. E-book. http://rogerjameshamilton.com/entrepreneurinspiration/

## CHAPTER 38

1. Hoffman, Reid, and Ben Casnocha. *The Start-up of you: adapt to the future, invest in yourself, and transform your career.* New York, Crown Business, 2012.

2. Hoffman, Reid, and Ben Casnocha. *The Start-up of you: adapt to the future, invest in yourself, and transform your career.* New York, Crown Business, 2012.

## CHAPTER 40

1. "The NCES Fast Facts Tool Provides Quick Answers to Many Education Questions (National Center for Education Statistics)." *National Center for Education Statistics (NCES) a Part of the U.S. Department of Education,* nces.ed.gov/fastfacts/display.asp?id=372

CPSIA information can be obtained
at www.ICGtesting.com
Printed in the USA
FFHW010737230119
50090093-54928FF